Against Free Speech

Polemics

Series Editors: Mark Devenney and Clare Woodford

Polemics draws on radical political philosophy and theory to address directly the various crises that have plagued global society and capitalism in the past decade. The series presents radical critiques of and alternative visions to the existing way of doing things. The texts in this series represent philosophically rigorous but polemical interventions in contemporary global, financial, political, environmental and theoretical crises.

The series is published in partnership with CAPPE, University of Brighton.

Titles in the Series

Kidnapped Democracy, Ramón A. Feenstra

Against Free Speech, Anthony Leaker

Against Free Speech

Anthony Leaker

ROWMAN & LITTLEFIELD
Lanham • Boulder • New York • London

Published by Rowman & Littlefield
An imprint of The Rowman & Littlefield Publishing Group, Inc.
4501 Forbes Boulevard, Suite 200, Lanham, Maryland 20706
www.rowman.com

6 Tinworth Street, London SE11 5AL, United Kingdom

Copyright © 2020 by Anthony Leaker

All rights reserved. No part of this book may be reproduced in any form or by any electronic or mechanical means, including information storage and retrieval systems, without written permission from the publisher, except by a reviewer who may quote passages in a review.

British Library Cataloguing in Publication Data Available

HB 978-1-78660-958-8
PBK 978-1-78660-855-0

Library of Congress Cataloging-in-Publication Data
Library of Congress Control Number: 2020941349

ISBN 978-1-78660-854-3 (cloth: alk. paper)
ISBN 978-1-78660-855-0 (pbk: alk. paper)
ISBN 978-1-78660-856-7 (electronic)

Contents

Acknowledgements	vii
Introduction	1
Free Speech Mania	1
Free Speech as Reactionary Politics	4
Free Speech Warriors	7
Notes	11
1 Make Liberalism Great Again!	13
The Liberal Centre	16
Reactionary Coalition	20
Enlightenment Roots	25
Notes	31
2 The War on Students	35
Students of Terror	38
Debate Fetish	42
Safe Spaces	46
Unprepared for the Real World	50
Notes	54
3 Racial Liberalism	59
Charles Murray	65
Hate Speech	73
Speech Acts	76
Notes	79

4	The War on Muslims	83
	What Is Islamophobia?	86
	Free Speech as Civilisational Discourse	89
	Charlie Hebdo and the Right to Offend	91
	Muslim Voices	98
	Notes	103
5	Silencing	107
	Power	110
	Notes	114
Bibliography		117
Index		127

Acknowledgements

Thanks to Mark Devenney for the initial impetus and support along the way.

Thanks to Gavan Titley and Nick Reimer for the incredibly helpful feedback and encouragement, and for being such sound dudes.

Thanks to all the reviewers.

Thanks to all my supportive colleagues on the Humanities Programme at the University of Brighton, especially Vicky Margree who has repeatedly gone above and beyond.

Thanks for the kindness, patience and support of everyone at Rowman & Littlefield—Frankie, Rebecca, Scarlett, Elaine, Brianna and Karen.

Thanks to the many people whose thinking and writing has informed the book's arguments, especially Anshuman Mondal, Aurelien Mondon and Aaron Winter, Arun Kundnani, Aziz Rana, Brian Leiter, Gurminder K. Bhambra, Charles W. Mills, Jennifer Peterson, Joe Kennedy, Kimberlé Crenshaw, Moira Weigel, Pankaj Mishra, Robin D. G. Kelley, Yassir Morsi, Wendy Brown, Adam Johnson and Nima Shirazi of *Citations Needed*, Daniel Denvir of *The Dig*, all at *Novara media* and Natalie Wynn of *Contrapoints*.

Special thanks to my mother for helping out so much with my children and in many other ways so I could get it written.

And very special thanks to my partner, Pati, for all the love, support, patience, and encouragement.

This book is dedicated to my children Clara, Ava and Sophie, and all the young people across the globe fighting to create a green, socialist future.

Introduction

FREE SPEECH MANIA

How can anyone be against free speech? What could it mean? To be in favour of censorship, controlled speech, policed and monitored speech? To support oppressive governments that imprison dissident protesters, writers and artists for expressing ideas deemed to be threatening to the State? Free speech, we are ceaselessly told, is the bedrock of democracy, of civilized society, of all that is great and good about mankind's social, cultural and political life and development—free speech is "a basic human right, and its protection is a mark of a civilized and tolerant society".[1] What rational person could possibly object to a universal value such as free speech? Without it, what would our society look like: an authoritarian police state?

Well, can we be sure that it doesn't already? More importantly, is the claim that free speech is the basis of liberal democratic society anything more than an empty dogmatic slogan, trotted out at every opportunity not to foster critical thinking, but like all dogmas, merely to induce conformism and torpor, and perpetuate the existing order of things? Even if it is, are liberal democracies such as Britain, France and the United States actually liberal or democratic in any concrete, meaningful sense? And are so-called civilized and tolerant societies really so civilized and tolerant, and are civility and tolerance all they are cracked up to be? If not, could free speech be part of the problem? And what is free speech anyway?

In the last few years, free speech has become a media obsession, so much so that free speech stories and free speech arguments are almost indistinguishable from parodies, such as when widely published, tenured professors with regular columns in major newspapers portray themselves as silenced victims.[2] There is a seemingly never-ending series of media accounts that consist of dire warnings or hysterical hand-wringing about its imminent demise; again and again we hear that there is a 'free speech crisis', that 'free speech is under threat' because the 'left' or 'students' or 'Muslims' 'hate free speech'.[3] Barely a week goes past without a free speech controversy of some kind hitting the news—usually related to something supposedly politically correct liberal elites have done to threaten free speech, and usually followed by privileged establishment voices barking boilerplate arguments by rote from their legacy media platforms.

Why have free speech and free speech issues become such an obsession, if not *the* obsession, of this post-crisis historical moment? Why in a period of political and economic turmoil, ongoing global conflicts, climate catastrophe and the mainstreaming of the far right has something so abstract come to seem so important? And why is it that those screaming most loudly about free speech are often those least likely to deliver it others? How is it that free speech has become such a pivotal tool for the growth of the far right, and how and why has the liberal centre been such a willing accomplice in this growth? Why in an era of real and dangerous threats to freedom more generally, such as rising authoritarianism, is there such an unhinged focus on the supposed threat to free speech posed by marginalised subjects such as students, Muslims, trans people and people of colour? And how is it that free speech continues to be viewed as speaking truth to power even when it is mostly used to stigmatise already disadvantaged minorities? And why, when the political right has always been and continues to be unashamed in its readiness to shut down free speech, are people on the left so willing to participate in propagating and supporting free speech crusades?

In attempting to answer these questions this book will argue that free speech is increasingly, and blatantly, being used as an ideological tool; a tool being weaponised in all sorts of ways by a range of political groups, organisations, institutions and public figures, including politicians, journalists and media celebrities, academics and professional trolls. These figures frequently invoke free speech to legitimise and justify their attention-seeking, intentionally provocative behaviour and statements, and have been very successful in doing so. Some have built entire careers and even a presidency on the use of divisive, racist, anti-immigrant rhetoric posturing under the guise of anti-political correctness and the right to offend.

The book is concerned with the use and misuse of free speech, and though it addresses the principle of free speech, it is primarily against arguments of principle. Getting drawn into arguments of principle is part of the problem, as they deflect attention away from issues of power, context and the specifics of each case. In this sense it is a Wittgensteinian argument. Wittgenstein argued in his later work that if you want to know what a word means, in most cases you need to know or look at how it is used. How, he asked, does it work in practice, and how do explanations of words work in practice? Asking abstract questions that attempt to provide pure or essential definitions will only lead to mental cramps.[4] Such definitions are misleading metaphysical theories that prevent us from seeing how language works in practice. By looking at how free speech is used, one can see what it means, and that its meaning has changed over time and across cultures; that its meaning is not fixed. And we will see that what it means today is very different from what it is commonly or theoretically perceived to mean.

The book is an argument against the use of appeals to principle that obscure, obfuscate, legitimise, and normalise the political and ideological, as well as harmful and damaging, ways free speech is used. To insist on defending free speech as an abstract principle is often a means of refusing to examine how it works in practice, of refusing to listen to the many criticisms that show that it is not doing what its defenders claim it is doing. It is not the preserve of the weak against the strong, or the poor against the rich, or non-white against white people. In most free speech controversies, we will find that certain voices will not be heard. Far from doing what free speech is supposed to do—foster open, rigorous debate between alternative positions and points of view—when free speech itself is invoked the effect is often to silence voices and views. And this, I will argue, is in part to do with the liberal underpinnings of free speech, due that is, to the fact that liberalism's conception of free speech, like most liberal rights, "has been—and still is—narrow and fragmentary, incomplete and biased and, all things considered, sordidly racist".[5]

By invoking principle, many free speech arguments tend to rely on speculative or hypothetical claims about how things would be without robust free speech legislation. This prevents consideration of the impact of speech, of what happens when hate speech, for example, is given a platform and legitimised. The focus on the abstract moral question of the right to free speech, or even on the limits of free speech, directs discussion away from more important issues concerning prominence—which platforms matter, which voices are heard, which voices and viewpoints dominate, what constitutes common sense, and who has the power to amplify voices. In order to understand this, we need to understand power, and how it operates in liberal democracies. And we need to understand the power of narratives.

FREE SPEECH AS REACTIONARY POLITICS

There are two main reasons to be against free speech. First, because of the way it has been weaponised to legitimise racist, sexist, transphobic, xenophobic and Islamophobic speech and action. Second, because of the ideological role it plays in legitimising liberalism as a ruling or hegemonic ideology.

The book will argue that free speech needs to be viewed as an ideological construct, and one that is used for distinctly unemancipatory political purposes. It is a rallying point for a number of diverse reactionary projects, such as defeating identity politics and political correctness on university campus, legitimising Islamophobia and discrediting Black political struggles. These projects need to be viewed as symptoms of grievance politics, of aggrieved liberalism, aggrieved maleness and aggrieved whiteness, that is to say, as forms of reactionary politics that blame the less powerful for the loss of, or challenges to, advantages previously regarded as entitled.[6] Free speech is a means of restoring "traditional cultural order",[7] its use and invocation needs to be viewed as part of a wider backlash against gains made by minority groups; a backlash on behalf of patriarchal white supremacy, with the support of the liberal establishment and significant numbers of people on the left.

Free speech is a central strand of a renewed culture war against progressive forces, which like all culture wars, relies on a set of powerful narratives, tropes, memes and bogeymen. Culture wars work "to direct attention away from the issues of the greatest substance, not towards them",[8] and likewise, free speech controversies coalesce into a series of dominant narratives that act as a smokescreen; they constitute a form of moral panic, manufactured to deflect attention from actual crises, and do so as a way of maintaining power. This book is an argument against these dominant free speech narratives, and the role they play in other ideological narratives: narratives that misrepresent and demonise students, people of colour and Muslims, and narratives that attempt to legitimise whiteness and the liberal establishment more generally.

Arguments in defence of free speech often masquerade as a concern for society in general when in fact they are a concern for a narrowly prescribed vision of, and set of people in, society. Free speech is most commonly invoked in order to defend and legitimise the status quo, to legitimise people who already have power against challenges to that power, and contrary to common conceptions, this has more or less always been the case.[9] For the far right and anti-PC liberals it is a key tool used to defend, perpetuate and promote patriarchal white supremacy and ethno-nationalism, it is used as a Trojan horse by which they infiltrate and undermine the public sphere.[10]

Free speech has become a tool for these reactionary political projects at the very time that democracies across the globe are becoming increasingly illiberal. On the surface this might make sense, since one clear indication of an illiberal state would be curtailed free speech: if, for example, dissidents were being rounded up and imprisoned for criticizing their governments. This is indeed happening in various parts of the world, including in countries perceived to be the torch-bearers of free speech—France, Britain and the United States. But this is not what you'll read about in stories and reports of the so-called free speech crisis. The pedlars of the free speech crisis narrative (who by now can be considered to constitute an industry) mostly have little interest in foreign authoritarian governments or the practice of their own plutocratic or neoliberal governments; they show little concern for the real and actually existing threats to liberal values and democracy, such as the marketisation of public goods, the erosion of civil liberties, the "unchecked, leviathan security state" and the securitisation and militarisation of public space, and the barbaric treatment of migrants and other vulnerable members of the community.[11] They are mostly preoccupied by students, Muslims, Black Lives Matter activists and social justice warriors.

Free speech is effective as a political tool because it is an empty and sacred ideal, but one that, contrary to how it is usually represented, tends to serve dominant power. In practice it is frequently deployed to mark a cultural, political or civilisational frontier between universal and particular—white and non-white, secular and Muslim, male and female—and, as such, is a central part of a broader legitimising ideology that works to silence and castigate the views, beliefs and practices of Others, such as people of colour, women and Muslims, while at the same time denying the positionality (such as the race, gender and sexuality) of normative groups and individuals. It does this most commonly through the 'free speech defence': the invocation of a set of arguments concerning the sanctity of free speech, such as 'commitment to free speech matters most when it involves ideas you strongly oppose' and other clichés, in order to deflect attention from substantive issues of power, discrimination or epistemic injustice. This book will examine and challenge both the tiresome reliance on these clichéd, endlessly repeated formulas and the summary dismissal of attempts to critique free speech. It will argue against the claim that language alone—whether speech, writing or rational argument—can overcome deep-rooted prejudices and structural inequalities.

Free speech arguments function to amplify and normalise racist, sexist, or Islamophobic voices, and often serve to place "the bigot on the moral high ground".[12] More importantly, they work to prevent challenges to entrenched structural, institutional and normalised racism, sexism or Islamophobia by denying or disavowing structural or power imbalances. Indeed, the free speech defence often inverts actual power relations—the people making racist claims assert their victimhood when called out for their racism, decry censorship while denying their critics a voice, and refuse to consider how the conditions or terms of communication are not only biased but structured in their favour. They use the universalising rhetoric of liberalism—freedom, openness, truth—and claim to be defending universal values—what's right and true and good—to obscure their own advantage.

To argue that the 'free speech defence' is racist or Islamophobic is not merely a matter of addressing obvious racist hate-mongers such as Richard Spencer, Geert Wilders or Tommy Robinson; career opportunists who invoke free speech in order to try to legitimise racist speech. With such people it is very obvious that free speech is being weaponised for self-serving purposes and that they have no qualms about suppressing the freedom of speech of the people they malign, let alone any interest in defending it. More insidious and powerful are the mainstream free speech defenders who insist they are not racist or Islamophobic, but are merely expressing their concern for the threat they perceive to the cherished values and ideals of liberal democracy or open and free debate or whatever other shibboleth they choose to invoke.

Though the loudest free-speech warriors tend to be libertarians or opportunist racists, arguably it is the more moderate voices—those found in the pages of major media outlets, such as the *New York Times* or the *Guardian*—who are more significant. My main argument, therefore, is with the liberal centre, and its complicity with the right, and it is against dominant narratives rather than particular individuals. The liberal centre is hegemonic; its values dominate the mainstream media and the public sphere more generally. It constitutes common sense. It is the unstated background of most, if not all, public, political and cultural discourse. And it does the most to police the boundaries of these discourses. It is characterised by an unstinting faith in liberalism. Liberals rarely feel the need to defend liberalism with arguments; an assertion usually suffices, such is the extent of liberalism's embeddedness in our everyday language, practices, institutions, customs and laws, where it is "assumed rather than interrogated". Because free speech issues and arguments almost always take place "within the confines of liberalism", argues Catherine Mackinnon, it is as if liberalism alone makes free speech discussions possible "rather than also creates some of these issues and limits the means of effectively grappling with them".[13] It is for this reason that this book is a critique of liberalism as much as it is of free speech.

FREE SPEECH WARRIORS

Free speech advocates typically fall into two camps—liberals and libertarians. Liberals are people who adhere to liberalism as a political philosophy, which is not the same thing as the way the term is commonly used in the United States to refer to left-wing progressives. Liberals believe in the individual rather than the collective, and the enlightenment ideals of moral autonomy, equality before the law and the rights of man. They look to thinkers such as Milton, Locke and John Stuart Mill as proponents of the view that freedom of speech is pivotal to a free society, but accept that there must be limits to free speech. Libertarians share many liberal assumptions but tend to be more extreme in their individualism, which operates as a guiding ideology, and their suspicion of the state, which they seek to keep to an absolute minimum. They tend to be "free speech absolutists" who insist that to be effective free speech must be unrestricted and unlimited, like gun ownership. They are fundamentalists, and like all fundamentalists, they are fanatical, blind, prejudiced and dangerous. But they are also well-funded, powerful and hugely influential, and arguably, they dictate the nature and terms of the free speech crisis narrative.

There are many points of convergence between liberals and libertarians, especially when it comes to free speech. Both rely on the central arguments of John Stuart Mill's *On Liberty*, which claims that free speech is a necessary prerequisite for: the pursuit of truth and knowledge; democracy to properly function; and persons to be genuinely autonomous. They also rely on a number of arguments concerning the negative effects of restricting free speech: the possibility of banning truth; the possible chilling effect leading to a fear of speaking one's mind freely; and the slippery-slope argument concerning the potential for governments to overreach in policing people's speech and the general difficulty of drawing the line between acceptable and unacceptable speech.[14]

Both have a purely formal understanding of free speech that fails to address how, in practice, who gets to speak, where and when are matters of power and are unequally distributed. For both, free speech is totemic, as it embodies a whole set of other values but also prevents closer scrutiny of those values. Both liberalism and libertarianism are powerful ideologies, and it is important to analyse both the underlying philosophical assumptions of each ideology as well as how each one is operationalised as propaganda. The most vocal, the most widely published and publicised of free speech crusaders mostly tend to be the same kind of people—white, male, privileged, establishment. This fact is not the grounds for an ad hominem attack, but it points to their structural investment in a white supremacist patriarchal system. It is not a coincidence that their identity—something they mostly disavow—matches the system they defend in their campaigns.[15]

One of their main arguments for the importance of free speech is that it is central to the development of thought and human progress, and yet the loudest proponents of free speech seem to have little interest in any of the intellectual or political developments of the last one hundred years or so. They argue that free speech is essential for challenging dogma, received opinion and entrenched ways of thinking. And yet they are stuck within a dogmatic, entrenched, reactionary conception of free speech, and ignore, dismiss or straw man many of this and the last century's most significant political, philosophical and theoretical developments—developments that have re-conceptualised how we might and can think about language, power and the human subject. Free speech is deemed essential for preventing totalitarianism and challenging religious dogma, and yet it has a sacred status, like that of religious dogma. Indeed, it is often discussed in the same pious and doctrinaire manner of religious discourse, and arguments justifying its importance consist of little more than tired clichés, "meaningless phrases",[16] and "stirringly enunciated platitude(s) as a substitute for real thought".[17]

One of the main problems with free speech arguments is the largely unexamined assumptions underlying them, assumptions about language, society, subjectivity, politics and knowledge. They presume that language and discourse are neutral or free of power, that society is fair and equal, that we all inhabit a 'marketplace of ideas' in which we are free to argue our beliefs and will all be heard and taken equally seriously. Free speech arguments presume that we inhabit an ideal liberal democracy of autonomous rational subjects, with a functioning political system unencumbered by corporate economic power or white supremacist patriarchal structural power. Accounts of the so-called free speech crisis rarely present social, economic, cultural or historical reasons for what they're describing, but instead rely on speculative, psychologising claims about stereotyped groups of people.

Hence, the force of their arguments has less to do with their inherent qualities than the way they are made. They are made by authoritative figures, published in major international publications, given disproportionate airtime on radio and TV, and are endlessly recycled throughout mainstream and social media. The arguments operate rhetorically and discursively to maintain free speech's sacred cow status, which means they are often accepted as an article of faith or dogma, and so prevent any objections. It does not necessarily matter that the arguments are empty, contradictory and hypocritical, if they are repeated frequently enough, loudly enough and in the right places they become true.

Each chapter, therefore, will be concerned with both the form and the substance of free speech arguments, with how free speech arguments operate hegemonically. Each chapter will focus on a particular dominant free speech narrative and examine the ways in which such narratives are what Jelani Cobb calls "self-serving deflection[s]", means of obfuscating deeper issues through a focus on abstract questions of principle or a manufactured crisis or ideal ideological enemies.[18]

Chapter 1 will examine the current crisis of liberalism and the liberal centre's reaction to it: their veneration of the "left behind" and blaming of identity politics for the failures of liberalism. It will consider the role free speech has played in contributing to the rise and success of the authoritarian right and the reactionary coalition liberals have formed with forces on the right. It will argue that liberals have conferred legitimacy on hate-fuelled, reactionary bigots, thereby normalising bigotry and paving the way for the far right's political rise and success. It will consider how free speech operates more generally within liberal democracy—what ideological work it performs and the significance of the historical roots of free speech arguments in liberal enlightenment thought. By examining key features of the history and theory of liberalism it will show the ways in which universal humanism, narratives of democratic freedom, and principles such as free speech have been used to justify a range of structures, practices and discourses which are anything but emancipatory.

Chapter 2 is a critical examination of the so-called free speech crisis in universities, and explores why the university has become a key battleground in the backlash against progressive politics. It will challenge the dominant media narrative of politically correct snowflake students, seeking to understand the reasons for the panic and terror that students seem able to induce in academics, journalists and politicians. It explores the obsession with 'debate' and ends by considering some of the actual threats to higher education and students.

Chapter 3 looks at free speech in relation to race and racism and focuses on the student protests against Charles Murray at Middlebury College. The Middlebury protests exemplify many of the salient issues in debates around free speech and race: a liberal class defending the status quo, whiteness and white supremacy, asserting tired clichés about the sanctity of free speech, reasoned debate and democracy, while refusing to acknowledge structural imbalances and how power operates or engage with challenges to the conditions of debate; an institution dismissing student concerns while "extending every courtesy to someone they considered a flamethrowing pseudoscientist";[19] an insistence that disrupting norms is considered illegitimate and yet defending (racist) norms is legitimate; and the mainstream media unquestioningly privileging some voices over others and perpetuating self-serving myths. The chapter ends with a critique of liberal conceptions of language and speech, outlining the major insights of critical race theory and feminist philosophy of language with regard to hate speech and harm.

Chapter 4 concerns Islamophobia and the way free speech operates as a civilisational discourse that helps to create and shore up self-serving distinctions between different kinds of societies and different groups of people. It will look at how Britain, France and the United States portray themselves as leading examples of liberty and equality, and do so in part through demonizing others, creating a supposed binary between us and them. Maintaining such a binary view of things has been and continues to be central to the self-sustaining mythology of liberal democratic states, in which free speech plays a crucial role. The two sides of these countries—the self-congratulatory narratives about freedom and equality and the brutal treatment of others—have to be viewed together. The chapter ends by challenging the specious idea of the right to offend.

The concluding chapter makes the case for censorship, silencing and other forms of language policing by arguing that, since they already exist, the question is not whether or not they are good things, but how they should be implemented. It will examine the outsized role of the First Amendment in free speech arguments and the way it is used to benefit corporate power and the economically powerful. And it will make the case for a conception of freedom different from that offered by neoliberalism as freedom from constraint.

NOTES

1. Nigel Warburton, *Free Speech: A Very Short Introduction* (Oxford: Oxford University Press, 2009), 1.
2. Niall Ferguson, "Join My Nato or Watch Critical Thinking Die", *Sunday Times*, April 14, 2019, https://www.thetimes.co.uk/article/join-my-nato-or-watch-critical-thinking-die.
3. For an account of just how hysterical, see the montage of news headlines in the first few minutes of the Contrapoints video essay, "Does the Left Hate Free Speech?", https://www.youtube.com/watch?v=GGTDhutW_us.
4. Ludwig Wittgenstein, *Blue and Brown Books* (Oxford: Blackwell, 1958), 1.
5. Aimé Césaire, *Discourse on Colonialism* (New York: Monthly Review Press, 2000), 37.
6. Angela Mitropolous, "B-Grade Politics", *Medium*, November 23, 2013, https://medium.com/i-m-h-o/b-grade-politics-6c5c9f48bf00.
7. Will Davies, "The Free Speech Panic: How the Right Concocted a Crisis", *Guardian*, July 26, 2018, https://www.theguardian.com/news/2018/jul/26/the-free-speech-panic-censorship-how-the-right-concocted-a-crisis.
8. Nick Reimer, "Weaponising Learning", *Sydney Review of Books*, June 12, 2018, https://sydneyreviewofbooks.com/weaponising-learning.

9. See Louis Michael Seidman, "Can Free Speech Be Progressive", *Columbia Law Review* 118 (2018): 1–30, https://scholarship.law.georgetown.edu/facpub/2038.

10. Liz Fekete, *Europe's Fault Lines: Racism and the Rise of the Right* (London: Verso, 2018), 99.

11. Liz Fekete writes, "The biggest threat to democracy lies in an unchecked, leviathan security state with its own meta-narrative of anti-extremism, the parameters of which protect the activities of the state and its security services from any reckoning". Ibid., 46–47.

12. Charles R. Lawrence III, "If He Hollers Let Him Go: Regulating Racist Speech on Campus", in *Words That Wound: Critical Race Theory, Assaultive Speech, and the First Amendment*, ed. Mari J. Matsuda, Charles R. Lawrence III, Richard Delgado and Kimberlé Williams Crenshaw (London: Routledge, 1993), 159, ebook.

13. Catherine A. MacKinnon, "Foreword", in *Speech and Harm: Controversies over Free Speech*, ed. Ishani Maitra and Mary Kate McGowan (Oxford: Oxford University Press), xvii.

14. Judith Wagner DeCew, "Free Speech and Offensive Expression", in *Freedom of Speech*, ed. Ellen Frankel Paul, Fred D. Miller Jr. and Jeffrey Paul (Cambridge: Cambridge University Press, 2004), 82–84.

15. I will argue that free speech crusaders misrepresent the objects of their critique or scorn: they over-generalise, caricature and conflate disparate positions. By referring to free speech crusaders and making a set of arguments against them I am aware that I am in danger of doing the same thing. The first thing to note, however, is that I am generalising about dozens of people, most of whom self-identify as free speech campaigners, rather than thousands or millions, and about people who really are similar in all sorts of ways. It is possible there are subtle nuanced differences between each free speech warrior's political positions on things, but my interest is in dominant narratives, tropes, themes and myths. I make no claim to be accurately representing the ideas of any particular individual.

16. Simon Lee, *The Cost of Free Speech* (London: Faber and Faber, 1990), 1.

17. Alan Haworth, *Free Speech* (London: Routledge, 1998), xiii.

18. Jelani Cobb, "Race and the Free Speech Diversion", *New Yorker*, November 10, 2015, https://www.newyorker.com/news/news-desk/race-and-the-free-speech-diversion.

19. Taylor Gee, "How the Middlebury Riot Really Went Down", *Politico*, May 28, 2017, https://www.politico.com/magazine/story/2017/05/28/how-donald-trump-caused-the-middlebury-melee-215195.

Chapter One

Make Liberalism Great Again!

To understand free speech, the importance of free speech and the claims made on behalf of free speech, we need to understand liberalism. And to understand the current obsession with free speech we need to understand that both liberalism and liberal democracy are in crisis.[1] Contrary to the dominant narrative that suggests that recent political earthquakes such as Trump or Brexit are the cause of this crisis, it is more helpful to view them as symptoms of it. The crises of liberalism and liberal democracy are closely tied in turn to the crisis of capitalism and neoliberalism, though this is rarely commented upon by liberal centrists. Indeed, the capitalist crisis of 2007–2008, from which only the very rich have benefitted, can be said to have partly caused the current crisis of liberal democracy. But only partly, because liberal democracies have been in crisis since at least the 1990s and what was perceived to be a technocratic neoliberal take-over of governmental politics leading to mass disengagement and disaffection. In *Post-Democracy* Colin Crouch argued that by the mid-90s liberal democracies across the global north were in crisis, with democracy a hollowed shell consisting of little more than periodic elections with rapidly falling participation. Democratic governments were no longer serving the people but only corporate and finance capitalism, and voter disengagement was at an all-time high.[2] The period of post-war settlement in which capitalism conceded to worker demands with relatively high wages, job security and a strong welfare system was over—dismantled by neoliberal deregulation, an empowered finance sector exploiting a consumer economy based on increasing amounts of debt and a gradual erosion of public services and belief in the public sector. Neoliberalism was initially a right-wing ideology enacted by Thatcher and Reagan in the 1980s, during which time there existed various forms of opposition to it, both nationally and internationally. By the mid-90s, however, it had become hegemonic, utterly embedded in institutions across the globe and deleteriously impacting all areas of social, cultural and political life.

Blair and other centrists differed from Thatcherites in their neoliberalism and embrace of free market corporate capitalism, by offering some concessions to a politics of social justice and social welfare with their "third way". However, they did so in a way that only empowered finance capitalism even more. Not only were their social reform programmes only trimming at the edges, but in order to carry them out they further entrenched neoliberal hegemony through schemes such as Private Finance Initiatives, which dismantled the public sector by putting institutions such as hospitals, schools and prisons in the hands of private corporations. Accompanying the social reforms was a somewhat self-congratulatory and superficial form of liberal multiculturalism, focusing on symbolic rather than substantive change, with which they tried to give a seductive veneer to capitalism. As we will see below it was this concession to social justice that liberal centrists would come to blame for our current political crisis rather than the more structural onslaught on the economic, legal and political system.

Though both the Iraq war and the financial crisis of 2007–2008 led to significant politicisation of the public sphere, to radical social movements such as Stop the War, Occupy and the 'movement of the squares', both the success and failure of these movements only increased dissatisfaction with liberal democratic structures, ideology and political parties. These movements as well as devastating austerity policies and a number of other factors contributed to the collapse of the centrist consensus and hegemony over electoral politics, most evident in the dramatic and rapid collapse of previously leading social democratic centrist parties throughout Europe.

Rather than viewing this collapse, and the related rise of right-wing populism and far-right fascism, as indicative of a problem with the policies and practices and underlying values of liberal centrism, let alone with rapacious neoliberal capitalism, centrists have cast blame on everything and everyone else. Everyone, that is, apart from themselves and the so-called left behind or white working-class. Rather than recognise that there might be a problem with liberal democracy or liberalism or ask whether countries such as the United States or United Kingdom have ever been truly democratic; rather than thinking that the rise of the far right is a "regressive reaction to the neoliberalism carried out by the 'extreme centre'",[3] an extreme centre that masked its technocratic tinkering and utter capitulation to finance capital with the mere rhetoric of liberal values. Rather than consider that people have become disillusioned with the false promises of liberal democracy and its underlying norms because of blatant betrayals of these values through: official lies used to justify illegal wars; assaults on civil liberties; the privatisation and drastic underfunding of almost all public services; rampant widespread deregulation leading to, among other things, gross corporate negligence and malfeasance, such as the Enron scandal or tragic disasters such as Grenfell towers; or a raft of other crimes, scandals and failures, none bigger than austerity policies. Rather than consider any of these things, liberal centrists' solution has been to double-down on liberalism, especially its more 'muscular' form. For centrists the problem is a misguided left's apparent obsession with identity politics; centrists blame the rise of the far-right on advocates of social justice and equality, who apparently don't appreciate the value of liberal norms and so just need to be told, repeatedly, why they are important.[4] They need lessons in what is right and the right way to go about things, and warnings about what might happen if; if, for example, free speech protection is eroded by regulations. Their primary solution to the ravages of neoliberalism and the evisceration of liberal democracy is to advance the cause of enlightenment values and untarnished liberalism: to make liberalism great again!

This in part explains their obsession with free speech. As they never tire of repeating, free speech is fundamental to liberal democracy, and for liberal centrists, attitudes towards free speech are one of the causes of, and solutions to, the current crisis. Free speech, they argue, is not only the foundation of democracy, but also the key to rescuing it. Jeffrey C. Goldfarb, for example, writes that "the fate of democracy depends on how we address the dilemmas of free speech".[5] It is because so many people fail to appreciate the importance of free speech, because free speech has been undermined, because political correctness has unfairly policed honourable white men from expressing their grievances (i.e., racism) that, according to them, we are in this mess in the first place. As we will see in the next chapter this partly explains why centrists are so preoccupied with students. Jonathan Haidt, one of the leading proponents of the view that students are anti-free speech, authoritarian snowflakes, opens a talk entitled the "Age of Outrage" by asking "what is happening to our country and to our universities?"[6] as if whatever it is, it is the same thing; as if Trump's onslaught on American Democracy, civic values and social justice is somehow equivalent to students' commitment to equality and inclusion, and campaigns against hate speech. Like other centrists sounding the democracy-in-peril drum, he is worried about the increasing political polarisation in the United States and fears that as a consequence of its "fine-tuned liberal democracy" is in danger of coming apart. He considers a number of reasons for this—the lack of a unifying common enemy (if only there were more wars! By which he seems to mean good, noble wars. He overlooks the never-ending war on terror and the way in which Muslims have been made into an ideal enemy); a more diverse media, but especially social media; immigration and diversity, which though he thinks they are "good things, overall", nonetheless have some negative sociological effects, most notably reducing social capital; and the more radical nature of the Republican Party. But his main focus is university students and their apparent indoctrination by what he calls bad identity politics, or intersectionality.

THE LIBERAL CENTRE

Haidt is one of the key players in the liberal centre, which includes other anti-PC (political correctness) liberals like Eric Kaufman, Mark Lilla and Matthew Goodwin, as well as slightly 'softer' centrists such as Blairite Yascha Mounk, all of whom echo many of Haidt's arguments and frequently invoke free speech as a rallying point for their primary concerns. They all share an unstinting faith in traditional liberalism, which they think needs to be revitalised; almost all are "white men credentialed by . . . establishment institutions";[7] all act as if they are the only adults in the room, making claims without need for evidence or relying on highly selective evidence, and present themselves as the voices of reason, "calling the people back" to the principles of liberal democracy. (Mounk is outraged that populists tell "outright lies" and yet has no difficulty being the executive director at the Tony Blair Institute for Global Change's Renewing the Centre team. Does he think lies that justify an illegal invasion of a country, leading to mass slaughter, destruction and decades of political turmoil, are somehow less serious?) Mounk argues that we need to teach people "why the principles of liberal democracy retain a special appeal. Teachers and professors should spend much more time pointing out that ideological alternatives to liberal democracy, from fascism to communism, and from autocracy to theocracy, remain as repellent today as they have been in the past".[8] For Mounk, not only is there no alternative to liberal democracy, but imagining any social or political alternative is an anathema or seemingly impossible—he, like other centrists, don't even bother arguing that there is no alternative to capitalism so deep-rooted is the presumption of its unassailability. This is not solely due to a poverty of political imagination and lack of faith in human enterprise. It is because the dominant forms of liberal historical memory and narratives offer little assistance for imagining such alternatives.

Navigating the waters of liberal centrism can be head spinning: liberals are both to blame and the solution; there's been too much liberalism and not enough; there are good and bad liberals, good and bad liberalism; there are muscular and soft liberals, conservative and left liberals and then centrists—liberal liberals perhaps. Bagehot in the *Economist* claims that "liberalism as a philosophy has been captured by a technocratic-managerial-cosmopolitan elite"; these are bad liberals, and a bad elite. He is a good liberal (and though he doesn't acknowledge this, part of a good elite). These good liberals blame (bad) establishment liberals, as if the good liberals, such as *Economist* columnists or white male academics and think tank wonks, are somehow not part of the establishment. Good liberals are anti-PC liberals who disparage cultural liberalism (which is bad), but promote political and economic liberalism (which is good). This good elite versus bad elite hypocrisy is exploited most flagrantly in the anti-elite shtick of both Brexiteers and Trump. Millionaires, bankers, corporate CEOs, landed gentry MPs—all banging the anti-elitist, working-class-hero drum. This anti-elite discourse is a disingenuous and performative trope used to cast blame on undeserving others while eluding it themselves. As Mondal notes, these anti-elitist elites "take offence at a supposed zealousness and excess that is foisted upon them by an apparently powerful, bureaucratized elite on behalf of minorities, even though this is nothing more than a figment of their imaginations because, first, they are themselves a part of that elite and, second, the 'authorities' therefore represent their own interests far more than those of minorities".[9]

Broadly speaking, the anti-PC liberals argue that there has been too much focus on equality and social justice, on satisfying the demands of minority groups such as gays, blacks, women and trans people, and as such the hard-working white man has been forgotten about. Hard-working white man (or the 'traditional working class') is understandably resentful and so we shouldn't be surprised if hard-working white man has voted for supposedly anti-establishment populist causes such as Brexit or Donald Trump. When hard-working white man does or says sexist or racist things, using his free speech, we need to show our understanding and support because it is not his fault. The fault, these liberals argue, is with people who insist on calling out racism and sexism; it is the fault of political correctness and metropolitan elite do-gooders, students and Muslims, trans-rights activists and Black Lives Matter. Unlike these people, hard-working white man is actually expressing legitimate grievances as well as valid claims about white identity—claims as valid as any made by historically marginalised and oppressed identity groups, such as Muslims or people of colour. Therefore, argues the *Economist*, politicians must address "the concerns of the left-behind as a matter of priority rather than luxuriating in the peccadilloes of the cosmopolitan elite".[10] The idea that "the best solution to poverty is less poverty" seems not to have occurred to liberal centrists, who are more interested in promoting these legitimate concerns, and who obsess over cultural matters at the expense of economic ones like the cartoon postmodernists they claim to despise.[11] Though they recognise the importance of economic factors—making occasional nods to structural inequality—they read these through the prism of cultural concerns. They may concede that there is a link between economic anxiety and racialised, anti-immigrant attitudes, but they see the latter as a reasonable explanation for and response to the former. Ultimately though, for them the cause of the rise of the far right is not gross economic inequality, political disenfranchisement, a racist, xenophobic, Islamophobic mainstream media and political culture fanning the flames of hatred with incendiary headlines and policies, it is intolerant social justice activists.

This is why liberal centrists' greatest grievance is against identity politics, the enemy of free speech, and according to them, one of the major causes of our current political nightmare. In this, as in other things, their views are in line with libertarians such as the collective at *Spiked* (one of the ironies about both centrists and *Spiked* is that for such avowed anti-conformist individualists their ideas are not only predictable but near identical. Talk about group think!) *Spiked*'s Brendan O'Neill argues that today's crisis is caused by "the failure of liberal thinkers over the past four decades to challenge the growth of identity politics, intellectual relativism, and a new intolerance";[12] Bagehot in the *Economist* claims "identity politics is the biggest challenge to liberalism's commitment to free speech and diversity of opinion since the red scare of the 1950s".[13] Meanwhile, Mark Lilla has devoted a whole book to the subject, in which he argues that Hillary Clinton lost to Donald Trump because of the left's concessions to identitarian concerns that have fractured a sense of a shared 'we', and joins the chorus of white men blaming America's ills on campus politics. He claims that "American liberalism has slipped into a kind of moral panic about racial, gender and sexual identity that has distorted liberalism's message and prevented it from becoming a unifying force capable of governing".[14]

One consequence of this interpretation of political events, this 'political fetish' with hard-working white man, is that anti-PC liberal centrists have increasingly taken the side of illiberal causes and groups of people, and taken against progressive causes. (Though, as we will see in more detail in chapter 3, in their Orwellian world it is anti-racists who are illiberal not white supremacists.) Thus, they argue that if politicians wish to beat back the far-right tide they need to "more openly cater to white concerns about cultural and demographic change".[15] (There is a curious contradiction here. On the one hand liberals argue that bad ideas can be defeated by good ones; that minds and opinions and political positions can be changed through hard-hitting reasoned debate—that's why free speech is so vital. And yet they imply that hard-working white man's views are not going to change or are not even changeable and hence need to be accommodated.) Though ostensibly they are arguing that their policy proposals, most of which revolve around an idea of 'inclusive nationalism', are for the purposes of defeating rising authoritarianism and far-right ethno-nationalism, in fact many of their arguments advance an ethno-nationalist narrative and worldview, making ethno-nationalist ideas respectable in the process.[16] And at the same time, they argue that both the liberal left and the far left are the main problem. Centrists expend more energy blaming the left than the far right. The fact that "white people are being radicalised at an alarming rate and in disconcerting numbers"[17] is less of a concern than the left's supposedly damaging obsessing with "identity politics, cultural appropriation and shutting down free speech".[18] They argue that Antifa are equivalent to, if not worse than the fascists they are attempting to defeat; that students protesting white supremacists are worse than white supremacy; that the term Islamophobia is worse than the devastating racist treatment of Muslims. Indeed, not only are they unconcerned by the "serious and urgent threat" that white supremacy poses "to our political stability, social cohesion and general security",[19] but think a restoration of a white liberal world order is the solution. And on this point, as on others, they can be seen to have formed a "reactionary coalition with conservative nationalism" as well as with the far right.[20]

REACTIONARY COALITION

These links between the centre and far right are not surprising, however, because the rise and "mainstreaming of the far right" in both the US and Europe has been enabled by the centre.[21] As Gary Younge notes, "While the violence may come from the fringes, the encouragement comes from the centre".[22] Indeed, in Europe the success of the far right has come about in part because, as Liz Fekete shows, "mainstream political parties have acted as facilitators" by, among other things, "implementing nativist and anti-Muslim policies and laws", and "by scapegoating refugees, Muslims, Roma and the 'indolent'". Since the early 1990s, argues Fekete, there has existed a "convergence of interests" between the centre and the far right around a whole range of issues, from the securitisation of immigration and asylum policies to the rationing of welfare provision to exclude migrants; to anti-multiculturalism with its focus on supposedly incompatible cultural values.[23] A similar pattern is evident in the United States. As Daniel Denvir and Thea Riofrancos explain, the "far right's fanatical demands are often for maximalist positions that the liberal order has already delivered". Challenging the liberal centre's depressingly commonplace argument that border controls and stricter immigration policies will somehow miraculously appease far-right xenophobia, they point out that "liberal complicity with border security and immigration enforcement have only galvanized the far right to demand more".[24] As Younge argues, "any concession that is made to bigots does not satisfy but emboldens them. That is, in no small part, how we got here".[25]

It is not only political parties that have acted as facilitators, but also the mainstream media. This is particularly evident in the negative coverage of Muslims and immigrants (as will be explored in chapter 4), but also in the normalising of the far right. Redoubtable establishment media outlets such as the BBC and the *New York Times* have consistently and favourably platformed a range of far-right figures from Nigel Farage and Marine Le Pen to Richard Spencer and Tommy Robinson.[26] As Nathan J. Robinson comments, "If you'd like to be the subject of a long, humanizing profile story at a major national magazine or newspaper, the quickest route to free publicity is to start espousing Nazism". The media has increasingly given extremists, "grindingly algorithmic alt-right controversialists"[27] and professional anti-PC trolls who desperately crave attention "precisely what they are looking for".[28] And free speech has been one of their primary tools for achieving this. Whenever so-called controversial speakers are invited onto mainstream platforms, or make objectionable statements, both their supporters and liberal centrists (often one and the same) will invariably invoke the importance of free speech, diverting attention from while simultaneously normalising the content of the given speaker's views. But it is important to note that far-right figures such as Nigel Farage or Tommy Robinson are accommodated on the platforms such as the BBC not in spite of their views but because of them. It is not merely that they generate heat, copy and increased audience share, more often than not their views accord with dominant, centrist views.[29]

And so we find ourselves in a situation in which not only are people more freely expressing racist hate speech, but they are expressing it as free speech martyrs or defenders of liberal democratic ideals, and getting increasing amounts of publicity and speaking opportunities for doing so. This gives more airtime to racist views, thereby normalising racism and potentially emboldening extremists to carry out racist attacks and spread their hatred. Furthermore, even if the hate speech is condemned the typical framing of such events helps perpetuate the idea that racism is a matter of bad people expressing offensive views, that it is the behaviour of extremists and therefore that liberals can't be racist, as they are not like those people—very often there is an explicit class prejudice here, in which racist behaviour is seen as the preserve of the so-called white working class. This can be the case even when the outrageous comments are made by highly privileged elitist figures such as Boris Johnson or Nigel Farage, who are somehow seen as men of the people, expressing 'populist' truths.

There is a great deal wrong with this anti-PC liberal picture of things; not least is the fact that it has gained such currency as to become the dominant narrative to explain authoritarian populism. The main problem with it is that hard-working white man only exists in the self-serving discourse of liberal centrists and the establishment media, and so-called white concerns are grossly misrepresented. White working-class people are represented as a homogenous group of nativist racists more interested in blaming their black or brown neighbour than the political and economic policies that have destroyed their communities and livelihoods. And so we are presented with a "one-dimensional portrait of provincials grounded in a simplistic, badly modelled opposition between them and metropolitan elites",[30] a portrait which is then relentlessly and cynically instrumentalised by another elite—the liberal centre—to advance its own dubious political agenda. This misrepresentation is not only unfair to working-class people, but also deflects attention from more insidious forms of racism and prejudice, as well as from all the non-white people who have been 'left behind'. Liberals claim that the 'left behind' need to be heard, that they have been shut out from political discourse and unfairly castigated as lumpen racists. But it is in part their assumptions that have created such a narrative in the first place, a narrative that has also erased the voices of the very groups of people most badly left behind—that is, ethnic minorities who, studies show, are the demographic most negatively affected by austerity in particular and neoliberalism more generally.[31] Not only are ethnic minorities not included in the category of the left behind, they are actually blamed for white hardship. Thus, both Trump and Brexit were commonly explained as being delivered by a white working-class backlash against the metropolitan elite's privileging of minorities due to identity politics. But as Gurminder K. Bhambra illustrates, such claims "are not supported by a thorough analysis of the available empirical evidence either in the UK or the US". Citing studies by a number of different researchers, Bhambra shows that the dominant narratives in both cases bear only highly partial resemblance to empirical facts. In the case of Brexit, data analysis shows that far from being the case that constituents from white working-class former industrial heartlands in the North made up the majority of Leave voters, as the media would have us believe, the vote to leave was disproportionately delivered by the "propertied, pensioned, well-off, white middle class based in southern England". In the case of Trump's election victory, such a distorted, even inverted, view of the actual voting demographic is even more pronounced. "Contrary to many understandings, the swing to Trump was carried not so much by the white working-class vote, but the vote of the white middle class, including college-educated white people".[32]

In both cases, however, the mainstream media put a "disproportionate weight on a single narrative thread" of disgruntled, angry white men, obscuring the role of the middle-class, the wealthy, political and economic elites, and the media themselves in bringing about such political results. There is a significant irony here, as liberal centrists, who disavow and disparage identity politics, have made identity politics the central strand of their analysis and their politics. Bhambra writes, "The return to 'class' via a focus on the white working class shows the purported concern with socio-economic realities actually to be a concern with a new identity politics of race—where 'whiteness' trumps class position".[33] They are claiming to be discussing class and repudiating identity politics, but in fact by viewing the left behind solely in terms of the white working class they are conflating socio-economic position with racialised identity. Such an apparent contradiction is enabled by their liberalist assumptions. As we will explore in more detail in chapter 3, in general white liberals do not consider whiteness an identity, indeed they often recoil at the idea; rather they tend to "view themselves as universal humans who can represent all of human experience".[34] But for now it is important to note that their assumptions concerning neutrality and their disavowal of structural power mean that centrists are attempting to argue that white majority claims are somehow equivalent to claims made by minority citizens, even though the latter "occurred in the context of conditions of structured racial inequality and as a means to redress that inequality, a redress argued for in terms of inclusive justice rather than partiality", whereas white claims are a consequence of a wish to exclude and to dominate. In the first case, "what is attributed as identity politics cannot be separated from an address of inequalities, while in the second case, identity politics are an expression of a wish to maintain those inequalities".[35] This helps to explain why liberal centrists are so threatened by and obsessed with dismissing identity politics, because what they are defending is their unquestioned position of superiority and privilege. Their attack on identity politics is a disguised form of white supremacy, or what Joshua Paul describes as "a cloaked identitarian politics which through a hegemonic narrative (re)presents itself as a radically inclusionary counternarrative".[36]

On a basic level, identity politics is the demand for equality and justice from groups of people who, on account of their group identities, have been socially, economically, politically and culturally excluded, oppressed and marginalised by dominant forces in a given society, forces that, among other things, thereby implicitly assert their own superiority while presenting themselves as inclusive, democratic and open to change. In other words, identity politics is at root a response to the normative order that projected a set of negative values onto these identities in the first place, not, as commonly argued, people insisting on the special importance of their particular identities (this specious line of reasoning is all too common in criticisms of Black Lives Matter).[37] If there were no historical mistreatment of people on account of their belonging to a group identity, there would be no identity politics. To be against identity politics, therefore, is very often to be against demands for equality and justice, and to be in favour of maintaining white male hegemony. In particular, it is to be against significant critiques of the idea that liberal democratic states based on liberal enlightenment principles can adequately provide equality and justice for marginalised groups without undergoing a radical transformation. This is not to say that identity politics is immune from criticism. Indeed, the history of identity politics is one of continual revision and reassessment in response to sustained criticism. However, there is an important distinction to be made between the criticisms of identity politics as it is practiced and theorised, and the criticism of identity politics when used, as it all too often is, as a punching bag to dismiss criticisms of dominant orders. Indeed, the best critiques of identity politics have been made by some of the very people, such as Judith Butler and Kimberlé Crenshaw, most commonly associated with identity politics. Radical identity politics is both misrepresented and conflated with what is actually liberal identity politics. What is today perceived as identity politics has very little to do with the identity politics of radical Black, LGBTQ or feminist liberation struggles. These liberation movements were either crushed out of existence or appropriated into a politically acceptable form of liberal multiculturalism that turned its focus away from structural changes to a politics of recognition. From the outset liberation movements that campaigned for equality, justice and inclusion were subject to a relentless backlash from across the political spectrum.

The real problem with identity politics, as with political correctness, affirmative action and all the other bêtes-noires of the anti-PC culture warriors is not that they somehow redistributed the balance of power so that the white man became an oppressed minority; it is that they were not effective enough. They were unable to fully uproot the deep underlying structural inequalities and forms of discrimination pervasive in liberal democracies such as Great Britain and the United States, nor hinder the devastating effects of racial neoliberalism. As Kalwant Bhopal and others have shown, white privilege is alive and well and thriving, as "vast inequalities between white and black and minority ethnic communities continue to exist".[38] White structural advantage and racial discrimination against people of colour is apparent in education, housing, employment and the justice system.[39]

ENLIGHTENMENT ROOTS

One of the significant features of contemporary centrist arguments against identity politics is how closely they resemble those of class-centric leftist arguments made in the 1990s, which were similarly based on an ahistorical appeal to abstract liberal principles. Writing in 1997, Robin D. G. Kelley summarised this 1990s critique as follows: "'The Left' has lost touch with its Enlightenment roots, the source of its universalism and radical humanism, and instead has been hijacked by a 'multicultural left' wedded to 'identity politics' which has led us all into a cul-de-sac of ethnic particularism, race consciousness, sexual politics, and radical feminism". Then as now establishment white men threatened by challenges to their position of dominance appealed to liberal enlightenment principles to justify dismissing or disparaging claims made by excluded minorities. And the problem with their argument is their narrow, historically selective, self-serving use and account of liberal enlightenment thought and principles. "These people assume", writes Kelley, "that the universal humanism they find so endearing and radical can be easily separated from the historical context of its making".[40] But a close examination of this historical context reveals that 'universal humanism' has been one of the most powerful tools for perpetuating and legitimising not only historical acts of barbarism—from slavery to colonial subjugation—but ongoing forms of inequality, exclusion and injustice. And it is only by understanding this history that we can understand the ideological way free speech operates within a liberal enlightenment framework, which is anything but equal, inclusive and democratic.

Mounk recognises that liberal principles "are often invoked insincerely", but thinks the right response to "such hypocrisy is to work even harder for them to be put into practice".[41] But what if this failure to realise principles is not merely hypocrisy but a structural and ideological feature of liberalism? What if the principles have always been invoked insincerely, but necessarily so? What if liberalism's multiple exclusions were, as Charles W. Mills argues, "theoretically central"?[42] For much of its history, liberalism has been exclusionary; though liberalism has "has prided itself on its universality and politically inclusionary character", writes Uday Singh Mehta, "liberal history is unmistakably marked by the systematic and sustained political exclusion of various groups and 'types' of people".[43] Exclusion does not solely mean not being allowed in. It means being turned into an 'other'; being dehumanized, which is crucial to the justification and legitimisation of the material subjugation and violence inflicted onto colonized subjects. This is why language and discourse is of such great importance, for as Patrick Wolfe notes "in historical practice, the ideology of race is intrinsically performative . . . rather than simply describing human groups, it brings them into being as inter-relating social categories with behavioural prescriptions to match".[44] As we will examine in subsequent chapters, words are not just ideas, but acts that play a crucial part in the creation of hierarchy and exclusion.

Liberalism has been structurally, ideologically and materially racist, sexist, xenophobic and heteronormative. It was at its origin, it has been throughout most of its history and it still is today, in part because of its seemingly inextricable tie to capitalism. Liberalism is the legitimising ideology of capitalism, its smiling face. It is the "ingratiating moral mask which a toughly acquisitive society wears before the world it robs".[45] However, this is not how liberalism is represented. Indeed, it is central to liberalism's conception of itself that it is neutral, egalitarian and values only the sexless, colourless individual. Mounk is right that we should all be taught that liberal democratic principles have a special appeal; they have a special appeal for people in and with power, for those supposedly unmarked universal agents of freedom—property-owning white men. What Mounk and others seem unable to consider is the possibility that these cherished principles might be part of the problem, that the principles themselves have served as ideological tools, used to legitimise a range of exclusionary, exploitative, extractive and oppressive policies and practices. Mounk acknowledges that the left has made some valid criticisms of liberal democracy. He writes, "Even though they aspired to universality, many Enlightenment thinkers wound up excluding large groups from moral consideration. Even though they have huge accomplishments to their name, many of the 'great men' of history committed horrifying misdeeds. And even though the ideal of liberal democracy is very much worth defending, its current practice continues to tolerate some shameful injustices".[46]

This apparent critique is little more, however, than a self-serving justification of liberalism's inviolability; it is a typical piece of 'yes, but' apologia, along the lines of 'yes, colonialism was bad, but it provided vital infrastructures'.[47] It implies that the faults of liberalism are contingent and accidental—aberrations—to do with certain thinkers or great men. Most liberals are not unwilling to recognise the 'chequered' history of liberalism. It would be hard not to, given the central role of slavery, colonialism, the genocide of indigenous peoples and systemic inequality in this history, but they tend to view these as part of a progressive narrative towards an inevitable, more inclusive egalitarian end point. Thus, if they recognise its highly violent, exploitative and exclusionary history at all, and some do not, it will be to show that liberalism itself was the solution to its own crimes—slavery ended because of liberalism, civil rights came about because of liberalism and so on. As Yassir Morsi argues, the West hides its colonial past by knowing it:

> Perhaps more than any other empire(s), it acknowledges its past sins. But more often than not its sins are not an explanation of the racialised structures of today's world. Rather the confession becomes a current proof of its self-reflexive greatness. It shows the willingness to criticise itself and be accountable, unlike the despotic Middle Eastern regimes. It is a wonderful act of self-idealisation. How often has the Western voice scorned the wrongs of its past while performing, interruptedly, the same superiority that marked its racism?[48]

Overall, liberal apologists for empire imply that the costs were worth it because of the benefits, as if both were experienced by a shared humanity, by colonisers and colonised alike. (In some cases, contemporary figures even try to defend some of these past crimes by, for example, calling for a reassessment of the benefits of colonialism. Indeed, colonial revisionism as well as uncritical celebrations of Western civilization and the enlightenment are central strands within the anti-PC-let's-hear-it-for-the-white-man narrative[49]—as Mishra notes, "Panicky white bros not only virulently denounce identity politics and political correctness . . . they also proclaim ever more rowdily that the [white] West was, and is, best".)[50] Such triumphalist, progressive accounts of liberal history tend to either systematically erase the histories of exclusion or obscure the depth of liberal imbrication with barbaric practices, and their significant structural legacy. As Morsi notes, "the victories of democracy and liberalism have not become universal and humanist truths and speech from thin air. They have come not only from a logic, a clarity of reason, or from noble self-reflection alone, but also from blood and slavery".[51] Slavery was not an anomaly in early liberal societies; it was "not something that persisted despite the success of the three liberal revolutions. On the contrary", shows Domenico Losurdo, "it experienced its maximum development following that success"; "slavery in its most radical form triumphed in the golden age of liberalism and at the heart of the liberal world".[52] Losurdo documents in great detail that it was not merely a matter of great men committing horrible misdeeds, but also justifying them. It is not only that 'great' liberals such as Locke and Mill and a host of others defended and justified barbaric practices such as slavery and colonialism and did so while simultaneously advocating liberal principles, it is also that some of the most vociferous defenders of liberal principles and practices tended to be those most ideologically attached to slavery and colonialism; and that, as Vann Woodward notes, "the barriers of racial discrimination mounted in direct ratio with the tide of political democracy among whites".[53] To argue that these great liberals' ideas reflected the routine white prejudice of the time is to ignore both that they were revolutionary thinkers, celebrated still for their enlightened, progressive theories, and that their racial ideas were not mere sideshows, but foundational for our existing social, economic and political structures.

Modern day racism, which is to say, categorisation according to a hierarchy of racial types, emerged from liberal enlightenment thought. It is commonly argued that racism is somehow a natural human characteristic, that divisions and differences between types of humans have always existed. Indeed, this argument is sometimes used to claim that liberalism and liberal democratic nations mark the beginning of the end of racism. For example, in the "Age of Outrage", discussed above, Jonathan Haidt approvingly cites E. D. Hirsch's claim that "the history of tribal and racial hatred is the history and prehistory of humankind. . . . The American experiment, which now seems so natural to us, is a thoroughly artificial device designed to counterbalance the natural impulses of group suspicions and hatreds".[54] This is not only questionable history and anthropology, but overlooks the specific kind of difference race thinking involves, and significantly idealises the "American experiment". As Wolfe argues, "the fact that people have differentiated between human collectivities does not mean that they have been imbued with the discursive formation that today we call 'race'. Indeed, the unexamined assumption that other forms of collective differentiation necessarily presuppose racial thinking is a prime example of the ideological process whereby race has been naturalised in Western culture".[55] What distinguishes white European race-thinking from other forms of conceptualising difference is that whiteness is conceived as the norm, and racial schema are always thought about in terms of difference from whiteness. Wolfe argues that "race itself is a distinctive configuration of ideological elements", and this configuration is a specifically European (or Eurocolonial) invention. "As it emerges in the late eighteenth century", he writes, "race is a classificatory concept with two general characteristics. First, it is hierarchical. Difference is not neutral: to vary is to be defective. . . . Second, it links physical characteristics to cognitive, cultural, and moral ones". And therefore "race provided categorical boundaries that ensured the exclusiveness of the bearers of the rights of man".[56] It was because of race that liberalism was able to marry two seemingly contradictory ideas—universalism and particularism. All men are created equal. But not all human beings are 'men', or count as men. As Mills shows, the social contract central to both liberal theory and liberal governance was in fact a "racial contract"; we the people meant we the White people. The racial contract, by "denying the personhood of blacks and restricting the terms of the social contract to whites", reconciled the contradiction between enlightenment liberalism's proclamations of the equal rights, autonomy and freedom of all men taking place simultaneously with "the massacre, expropriation, and subjection to hereditary slavery of men at least apparently human".[57]

It is not merely a case, therefore, of a past failure to live up to the ideals of liberty. As Aziz Rana argues, far from being a contingent aspect of liberalism, in the case of America, racial exclusion and subjugation were integral to its liberal conception of liberty. He writes, "the democratic ideals themselves gained strength and meaning through frameworks of exclusion. Projects of territorial expansion and judgments about who properly counted as social insiders helped to generate and sustain the very accounts of liberty".[58] Thus the promise of liberty was historically linked to practices of racial subordination. This history is often overlooked or ignored, in part because of a tendency to only focus on the internal characteristics of American settler society, which means that "many commentators never confront the extent to which [America's] democratic ideals were themselves produced and sustained by colonial domination".[59] This limited focus is made all the more effective by the myths of exceptionalism, constitutionalism, and democratic equality which make a historical record riddled with ethnic, racial, and sexual exclusion easy to disregard, and help produce and sustain an ideological fantasy of freedom, and of liberal democracy as free of inequality. This narrow, idealising focus and ideological fantasy is in clear evidence in Haidt's "Age of Outrage", which invokes the Founding Fathers and their creation of a "fine-tuned liberal democracy", that its inheritors, modern day Americans, are merely meant to maintain, but not challenge or transform, such is its presumed state of ideal perfection.[60] For Haidt and many others, the constitution and associated democratic institutions are presented as gifts from mythic founders—and therefore as "outside the bounds of popular contest or continued struggle".[61] And there is no greater or more mythic gift than the first amendment and the right to free speech, which often function tautologically: free speech is sacred because the first amendment says so.

These issues are not solely a matter of a "distant period of conquest and subordination"; Rana shows that settler exclusion "provided the basic governing framework for American life for over three centuries",[62] and how exceptionalism and constitutionalism reinforce the inevitability and legitimacy of governing practices. This logic is not unique to America, however, but can be seen more broadly in colonialist ideology. In European imperialism, the Enlightenment idea of the human is also reduced to the figure of the settler colonial white man, and the brutality meted out to colonised subjects was equal to that inflicted on slaves. As W. E. B. Du Bois writes: "There was no Nazi atrocity—concentration camps, wholesale maiming and murder, defilement of women or ghastly blasphemy of childhood—which Christian civilization or Europe had not long been practicing against coloured folk in all parts of the world in the name of and for the defence of a Superior Race born to rule the world".[63] In other words, as Mills argues, "White supremacy is the unnamed political system that has made the modern world what it is today".[64]

It is vital, therefore, to understand that the democratic and Enlightenment ideals that are so frequently appealed to in free speech discourse and that form the basis of arguments in defence of free speech are not only ideological, but discriminatory and exclusionary, and still in operation today. The idea that citizens in contemporary liberal democracies enjoy equal and far-reaching freedoms is an ideological fantasy, and does a great deal of work to maintain existing power relations.[65] It is a form of whitewashing. By imagining politics as a marketplace of ideas in which all voices are legitimate and equal, one dissolves any need to account for centuries of structural inequality. This whitewashing of racial issues has a long history, and it has not ceased. The idea that today's liberal democracies are post-racial, colour-blind neutral spaces of equal opportunity is not only a myth, but a racist myth. Indeed, such a narrative is a very powerful racist tool. Mills writes, "illicit white racial advantage is still being secured, but now primarily through the evasions in [liberalism's] key assumptions rather than the derogation of nonwhites". In other words, though most white liberals vehemently disavow racism, the "liberalism they are endorsing is still racialised".[66] As we will see in subsequent chapters, the myths of liberal democracy and universal humanism serve a range of racist and Islamophobic ideologies and practices.

NOTES

1. See Bagehot, "Some Thoughts on the Crisis of Liberalism—and How to Fix It", *Economist*, June 12, 2018, https://www.economist.com/bagehots-notebook/2018/06/12/some-thoughts-on-the-crisis-of-liberalism-and-how-to-fix-it. See also Patrick J. Deneen, *Why Liberalism Failed* (New Haven, CT: Yale University Press, 2018.
2. Colin Crouch, *Post-Democracy* (London: Polity, 2004).
3. George Souvlis, "Marxism, the Far-Right and the Antinomies of Liberalism: An Interview with Enzo Traverso", Verso Books blog, https://www.versobooks.com/blogs/4296-marxism-the-far-right-and-the-antinomies-of-liberalism-an-interview-with-enzo-traverso.
4. Eric Kauffman, "How Progressivism Enabled the Rise of the Populist Right", *Quillette*, May 27, 2019, https://quillette.com/2019/05/27/how-progressivism-enabled-the-rise-of-the-populist-right.
5. Jeffrey C. Goldfarb, "Free Speech Matters vs. Black Lives Matter", *Public Seminar*, September 29, 2017, http://www.publicseminar.org/2017/09/free-speech-matters-vs-black-lives-matter.
6. Jonathan Haidt, "The Age of Outrage", *City Journal*, December 17, 2017, https://www.city-journal.org/html/age-outrage-15608.html.
7. Jedediah Purdy, "Normcore", *Dissent*, Summer 2018, https://www.dissentmagazine.org/article/normcore-trump-resistance-books-crisis-of-democracy.
8. Yascha Mounk, "How Populist Uprisings Could Bring Down Liberal Democracy", *Guardian*, March 4, 2018, https://www.theguardian.com/commentisfree/2018/mar/04/shock-system-liberal-democracy-populism.
9. Anshuman A. Mondal, *Islam and Controversy: The Politics of Free Speech after Rushdie* (London: Palgrave Macmillan, 2014), 28.
10. Bagehot, "Some Thoughts".
11. Joe Kennedy, *Authentocrats* (London: Repeater, 2018), 10.

12. Brendan O'Neill, "From No Platform to Safe Space: A Crisis of Enlightenment", in *Unsafe Space: The Crisis of Free Speech on Campus*, ed. Tom Slater (London: Palgrave, 2016), 9.
13. Bagehot, "Some Thoughts".
14. Mark Lilla, "The End of Identity Liberalism", *New York Times*, November 18, 2016.
15. Zack Beauchamp, "The New Reactionaries", *Vox*, February 26, 2019. https://www.vox.com/policy-and-politics/2019/2/26/18196429/trump-news-white-nationalism-hazony-kaufmann.
16. Beauchamp, "New Reactionaries".
17. Gary Younge, "White Supremacy Feeds on Mainstream Encouragement. That Has to Stop", *Guardian*, April 5, 2019, https://www.theguardian.com/commentisfree/2019/apr/05/white-supremacy.
18. Pankaj Mishra, "The Mask It Wears", *London Review of Books*, June 21, 2018, https://www.lrb.co.uk/v40/n12/pankaj-mishra/the-mask-it-wears.
19. Younge, "White Supremacy".
20. Beauchamp, "New Reactionaries".
21. Aurelien Mondon and Aaron Winter, "Understanding the Mainstreaming of the Far Right", *openDemocracy*, August 26, 2018, https://www.opendemocracy.net/en/can-europe-make-it/understanding-mainstreaming-of-far-right.
22. Younge, "White Supremacy".
23. Liz Fekete, *Europe's Fault Lines: Racism and the Rise of the Right* (London: Verso, 2018), 28–33.
24. Daniel Denvir and Thea Riofrancos, "Zombie Liberalism", *n+1*, April 11, 2018, https://nplusonemag.com/online-only/online-only/zombie-liberalism.
25. Younge, "White Supremacy".
26. Lynsey Hanley notes that "Ann Coulter, the far-right American columnist, has appeared several times on *Newsnight* over the last decade, called on to disparage the Black Lives Matter movement and defend Donald Trump. Nigel Farage has been on *Question Time* 32 times since 2000, even though Ukip has never had more than two MPs and Farage has never been one of them. *Newsnight*'s 'Viewpoint' strand recently described Tommy Robinson's supporters not as neo-Nazis but as 'the people fighting to free' the EDL leader. Raheem Kassam, the former Breitbart editor and author of a book entitled *Enoch was Right*, defended Robinson on the *Today* programme without challenge"—Lynsey Hanley, "Airtime for Hitler", *LRB blog*, August 8, 2018, https://www.lrb.co.uk/blog/2018/august/airtime-for-hitler.
27. Stewart Lee, "Why Greta Thunberg Is Now My Go-to Girl", *Guardian*, April 28, 2019, https://www.theguardian.com/commentisfree/2019/apr/28/why-greta-thunberg-is-now-my-go-to-girl.
28. Nathan J. Robinson, "Let's Just Stop Writing Long-Form Profiles of Nazis", *Current Affairs*, November 27, 2017, https://www.currentaffairs.org/2017/11/lets-just-stop-writing-long-form-profiles-of-nazis.
29. Equally if not more damaging than the high-profile figures, however, are the less well-known ideologues masquerading as experts frequently given airtime on major news programmes or platforms. For example, Frank J. Gaffney, a notorious Islamophobe and disseminator of multiple fake stories about Islam, has appeared on the BBC as an expert on Islam.
30. Kennedy, *Authentocrats*, 11.
31. Wendy Brown writes, "Neoliberalism, and post-Fordism before it, have been far more devastating to the Black American working class. In 1970, more than two-thirds of urban Black workers had blue-collar jobs; by 1987, that had dropped to twenty-eight percent. In addition to rising un- and underemployment, poor and working class Black neighborhoods were hard hit by neoliberal defunding of public schools, services, and

welfare benefits, and draconian sentencing mandates for non-violent crimes. Together, these resulted in an exploding drug and gang economy, a catastrophic Black incarceration rate, and a growing chasm between the possibilities for a small Black middle class and the social, economic, and political abandonment of the rest of African America"—Wendy Brown, "Neoliberalism's Frankenstein: Authoritarian Freedom in Twenty-First Century 'Democracies'", *Critical Times*, 1, no. 1 (2019): 60–61.

32. Gurminder K. Bhambra, "Brexit, Trump, and 'Methodological Whiteness': On the Misrecognition of Race and Class", *British Journal of Sociology* 68, no. S1 (2017): 215.

33. Ibid., 216.

34. Robin DiAngelo, "White Fragility", *International Journal of Critical Pedagogy* 3, no. 3 (2011): 59.

35. Bhambra, "Methodological Whiteness", 220.

36. Joshua Paul, "'Not Black and White, but Black and Red': Anti-identity Identity Politics and #AllLivesMatter", *Ethnicities* 1, no. 19 (2019): 16.

37. Ibid.

38. Kalwant Bhopal, *White Privilege: The Myth of a Post-racial Society* (Bristol, UK: Policy Press, 2018), 1.

39. Bhopal notes that "In the UK if you are from a black minority background you are three times more likely to be excluded from school, more likely to be unemployed, more likely to live in poverty, more likely to be physically restrained in police custody and more likely to be prosecuted and sentenced"—Bhopal, *White Privilege*, 9.

40. Robin D. G. Kelley, "Identity Politics and Class Struggle", *New Politics* 6, no. 2 (Winter 1997), available at https://libcom.org/library/identity-politics-class-struggle.

41. Mounk, "Populist Uprisings".

42. Charles W. Mills, *Black Rights/White Wrongs: The Critique of Racial Liberalism* (Oxford: Oxford University Press, 2017), xiv.

43. Uday Singh Mehta, *Liberalism and Empire: A Study in Nineteenth-Century British Liberal Thought* (Chicago: University of Chicago, 1999), 45.

44. Patrick Wolfe, *Traces of History: Elementary Structures of Race* (London: Verso, 2016), 34.

45. Cited in Mishra, "Mask".

46. Mounk, "Populist Uprisings".

47. For a recent example of this, see Dominic Sandbrook, "Of Course Slavery Was Abhorrent. But Cambridge Dons Who Now Feel Guilty about Our Empire Are Narcissistic Cowards", *Mail Online*, May 1, 2019, https://www.dailymail.co.uk/debate/article-6978591.

48. Yassir Morsi, *Radical Skin, Moderate Masks: De-radicalising the Muslim and Racism in Post-racial Societies* (London: Rowman & Littlefield, 2017), 7.

49. For evidence of this trend, see Nigel Biggar, "Don't Feel Guilty about Our Colonial History", *Times*, November 30, 2017, https://www.thetimes.co.uk/article/don-t-feel-guilty-about-our-colonial-history. For a trenchant critique of it, see Nick Reimer, "Weaponising Learning", *Sydney Review of Books*, June 12, 2018, https://sydneyreviewofbooks.com/weaponising-learning.

50. Pankaj Mishra, "The Religion of Whiteness Becomes a Suicide Cult", *New York Times*, August 30, 2018.

51. Morsi, *Radical Skin*, 6.

52. Domenico Losurdo, *Liberalism: A Counter-History* (London: Verso, 2014), 35, 37.

53. Cited in Wolfe, *Traces*, 42.

54. Haidt, "Outrage".

55. Wolfe, *Traces*, 26.

56. Ibid., 27.

57. Charles W. Mills, *The Racial Contract* (Ithaca, NY: Cornell University Press, 1997), 64.
58. Aziz Rana, *The Two Faces of American Freedom* (Cambridge, MA: Harvard University Press, 2010) 7.
59. Ibid., 10.
60. Haidt, "Outrage".
61. Rana, *Two Faces*, 6.
62. Ibid., 13.
63. W. E. B. Du Bois, *The World and Africa* (New York: International Publishers, 1947), 23.
64. Mills, *Racial Contract*, 1.
65. Jennifer Peterson, "Freedom of Expression as Liberal Fantasy: The Debate over *The People vs. Larry Flynt*", *Media, Culture & Society* 29, no. 1 (2007): 380.
66. Mills, *Black Rights/White Wrongs*, xv.

Chapter Two

The War on Students

One of the primary sites of the renewed interest in free speech is the university, which has become, yet again, one of the key battlegrounds of the latest iteration of the culture wars or the backlash against progressive politics. Why is this? Why are so many people—from media commentators to politicians to major financial players to Joe public—so concerned about what goes on in universities?[1] For much of the time, the mainstream media and general public are unconcerned with what goes on in universities: They are commonly viewed as privileged sites of indulgent impractical navel-gazing, irrelevant to the social, political and economic maintenance of society; dismissed as ivory towers, out of touch with the real world, rarefied playgrounds for academics to pursue jargon-filled, pointless research and students to explore pleasurable or political pursuits of no seeming consequence. And yet if liberal and conservative commentators are to be believed, then recent developments in universities could lead to the death of civilisation. The rhetoric used to describe such developments would suggest there is no institution more important for our future societies. Brendan O'Neill, for example, claims that "what we are witnessing in the academy today is something far more serious than the arrival of a coddled generation—we're seeing the end result of the corrosion of Enlightenment values, of Western societies' abandonment of the ideals of autonomy and subjectivity upon which university life, and democratic life, have been based in the modern period".[2]

The fact that a variety of social and political forces are so invested in challenging what goes on in universities is testament to their importance, and it is worthwhile examining why they are important, both in general and to right-wing conservatives and libertarians in particular, because only then can we attempt to understand the incredible overreaction in parts of the media to some of the things that have been happening on campuses. If tertiary education were not socially, politically and economically significant, neither the press nor governments nor think tanks would care what goes on in universities. So why are they considered to be important? Firstly, universities, or at least the elite ones, are considered to be the breeding ground for future leaders—leaders in politics, the law, media, business and cultural production.[3] Mark Lilla argues that universities are important politically because they educate the professional classes from which future liberals will be drawn. "Liberalism's prospects", he writes, "will depend in no small measure on what happens in our institutions of higher education".[4] And the liberal establishment evidently fears future leaders with different or challenging ideas to the status quo. Key establishment players may profess to want challenging, innovative critical or creative thinkers—this, they claim, is one of the reasons why free speech matters so much—but, as we will see, in reality they only want tinkering at the margins, which is unsurprising since the whole point of the establishment is to maintain itself. We frequently hear establishment figures advocating the importance of dissent or the need to interrogate one's 'unexamined beliefs', but such claims are deeply disingenuous, not least because of their investment in maintaining power.[5] How else explain the banal and dispiriting homogeneity of leaders in almost all spheres. Secondly, universities are perceived to be important for creating a productive, efficient workforce; and thirdly, for helping to produce an informed citizenry, and therefore, in maintaining civic society and values. PEN America states that the university is "an essential foundation for building a stronger and more open American society",[6] which, like many grandiose liberal statements, is somewhat question begging. More open for whom, minorities or corporations? Stronger how: economically, militarily, morally? For libertarians "stronger" and "open" mean very different things than they do to socialists. Such a vague formulation does, however, testify to the fact that the university is a highly contested terrain; that universities are and always have been an ideological battleground. Universities matter, notes Kimberlé Crenshaw, because they are not "apolitical arbiters of neutral knowledge" but significant "participants in the struggle over how social power is exercised".[7] And it makes sense that this struggle will be particularly heated in times of social and political crisis. For Will Davies, the university is currently a particularly heated battleground because it is the one area not completely taken over by neoliberal market logics, and so is seen as an untapped enclave not only for investment, but also for ideological take-over.[8]

But none of these reasons fully accounts for the extent and level of hysterical attention given to student demands and protests. It does not explain why politicians and the mainstream media seem to be so obsessed with free speech on campus. Is a student refusing to share a platform with Germaine Greer really such a threat to democracy? Democracy is under threat, about that there can be no question. But on the scale of threats to democracy how high can university safe spaces and no-platforming rank? They are not even the biggest threat to democracy in universities.

For the concerned commentariat, the problem is not the development of universities into corporate sausage factories or the sector into a competitive market or that higher education is, as Malcolm Harris notes, an "economic regime that extracts increasingly absurd amounts of money from millions of young people's as-yet-unperformed labour" leading to crippling debt and its damaging personal and social consequences.[9] No, the problem is the students—a supposedly mollycoddled generation of dangerous zealots. According to a tired but surprisingly pervasive and shatterproof narrative, there is a generation of fanatical, ideologically driven students intent on shutting down the noble pursuit of truth, knowledge and the good. For the last few years, barely a week has passed without the mainstream media warning that free speech on campus is under threat.

If the media-hype is to be believed, then universities are sites of incredible power and influence, with students holding almost all the power; seemingly as powerful as leading politicians, media moguls and corporate leaders, able to carry out a "new McCarthyism".[10] And what is the source of this power? How is it that a group of people who rarely get heard, let alone listened to, who have little-to-no financial or political power or influence, are deemed to be so threatening? How is it that a group of people who are deemed to be snowflakes—fragile, emotional, hypersensitive, overprotected idealists—and frequently told they need to toughen up, are seen to be so terrifying? Indeed, are seen as "authoritarian", as fascists, as bullies, as a threat not only to democracy, but civilisation.[11]

STUDENTS OF TERROR

Well, according to Edward Schlosser's "I'm a liberal professor, and my liberal students terrify me", a *Vox* article that became a minor online sensation, the fear of students is to do with the chilling effect of their supposedly self-righteous hypersensitivity to offence. Schlosser's primary concern is to show how personal experience and emotions have come to replace reason as the arbiters of truth and justice, and "safety and comfort have become the ends and means" of university experience.[12] Schlosser's article is one of many similar articles criticising students, written mostly, though not exclusively, by well-meaning liberals; mostly, though not exclusively, white male middle-aged liberals—some of whom haven't stepped foot on a university in decades, though this doesn't stop them holding forth as if they were informed experts on exactly how things are in universities and what universities are for. Indeed, the last few years has seen a flood of articles and books attacking students and, often, by association, the entire generation of millennials (the two are frequently conflated). And it is worthwhile examining how these articles function, what purpose they serve, and what is the basis, if there is one at all, of their claims.

Most of them will tell you what's wrong with students, they will repeat the same hoary clichés, they will make general claims about the dangers and consequences of privileging emotion over reason and about the rise of offence as the arbiter of all things, stating that: "the feelings of individuals are the primary or even exclusive means through which social issues are understood and discussed"; "students refuse to countenance and engage with uncomfortable ideas"; students have "a simplistic, unworkable and ultimately stifling conception of social justice";[13] and "have become dangerously thin-skinned".[14] They claim that "robust critical thinking skills" and the "vitality of participatory democracy" are under threat;[15] and that "there is now a student generation raised permissively and seldom challenged in its beliefs, and hence uniquely unready to face the clash of ideas which has always been the theoretical core, but less so the practical reality, of higher education"; that "like their pro-Nazi and pro-McCarthy counterparts, it is sufficient to declare that the victim is a Jew—or a Communist—or a "racist" or a "sexist".[16]

The first thing to note about these articles is the sheer quantity of them, which in itself does a lot of ideological work.[17] Propaganda and media bias are matters of preponderance and emphasis, not lies, though even with lies we know that if they are repeated often enough then they can become perceived as truth. Each article or report is like a self-replicating virus, producing ever more iterations of more or less the same story—stories that get repackaged on multiple platforms and then sediment into bite-size clichés. It has become metonymic, for example, that students are snowflakes. So, although plenty of dissenting accounts exist, they rarely get heard, they are drowned out and do little to challenge the dominant narrative. The second thing to note is the hysterical pitch—the issue is discussed in exaggerated and at times near apocalyptic terms, with frequent references to "Nazism"; "McCarthyism"; "Stalinism"; "totalitarianism"; "Salem witch hunts" or the "chilling", "death" and "killing" of free speech and how this is "dangerous" and an "epidemic".[18] Some even go so far as to equate student protestors with Islamic terrorists: "where No Platform protesters seek pre-emptively to shout down or shut down speakers they find offensive, the Copenhagen gunman sought to shoot them down. That is an important tactical difference. But the underlying attitude of intolerance of offensive speech seems familiar".[19] By portraying students as fanatics, critics are using a tried-and-tested tactic, for as Alberto Toscano notes, "One of the foremost 'uses' of the idea of fanaticism has been to cement and lubricate domination, inequality and privilege by holding up the threat of extremist upheaval against any movement for greater equality and popular control".[20] Third is misrepresentation: Each article uses similar rhetorical tropes and recycles the same anecdotes or controversies, which are cherry-picked as if they are typical and representative when often they are anything but. They are stripped of context and exaggerated and used as the basis for broad generalisations. And in quite a few cases they turn out to be completely untrue.[21] Finally, almost all such reports are characterised by the dismissal of the actual issues, they rarely report what it is that students are demanding or protesting about. As Jon Gould notes, media coverage is more interested in "pushing back on a presumed wave of political correctness that's allegedly threatening free speech on campus and beyond" than focussing "on the issues that generated the student demonstrations and protests".[22] In the few cases when they do focus on the issues, they choose one minor aspect, fail to properly contextualise it, and use it as a means of diminishing or ridiculing the protest.[23]

The overall impact of such reports is a highly effective campaign, a campaign that has all the features of a moral panic, and which is effective in spite of the fact that the claims have been repeatedly challenged from a number of reliable and reputable sources, which is to say, liberal establishment sources largely sympathetic to the free speech cause. A UK government commission, for example, concluded that there's no free speech crisis on campus—"evidence suggests that the narrative that 'censorious students' have created a 'free speech crisis' in universities has been exaggerated";[24] data analysis from Georgetown University's Free Speech Project suggests that "this 'crisis' is more than a little overblown";[25] and PEN America's free speech on campus report concluded that while "there have been some troubling instances of speech curtailed, these do not represent a pervasive 'crisis' for free speech on campus".[26]

Such evidence-based conclusions, though useful, should not be necessary, as it is patently obvious that this is a managed and concerted campaign, and a manufactured crisis.[27] It is part of a new culture war, the latest iteration of "political correctness gone mad" being wielded as a propaganda tool to help maintain cultural and political hegemony. Many of the tactics, tropes and arguments have been seen before—it is the same playbook from the culture wars of the late 1980s and early 1990s when universities were targeted by the anti-PC brigade in what was in part a carefully orchestrated and well-funded campaign. The introduction to *Words That Wound* from 1993 gives a sense of just how similar this playbook is. The authors show how defenders of the status quo weaponised free speech as part of "an emerging and increasingly virulent backlash against the extremely modest successes achieved by communities of colour, women, and other subordinated groups" on campus, a backlash that used "words like intolerant, silencing, McCarthyism, censors, and orthodoxy . . . to portray women and people of colour as oppressors and to pretend that the powerful have become powerless". These suddenly powerless white men portrayed themselves as oppressed by "leftist speech police . . . afraid to raise controversial issues, use humour in their classes, or express friendliness toward their students for fear of being called a racist, a sexist, or a homophobe by 'oversensitive' students".[28]

Behind many of today's stories of the supposed free speech crisis on campus lies a crusade driven by well-funded libertarian organisations such as *Spiked*, an online magazine dedicated to free speech advocacy, Campus Reform, a conservative news website, or the Foundation for Individual Rights in Education (FIRE), which purports to protect 'free speech' on campus, but, argues Jim Sleeper, "expends more energy blaming 'politically correct' activists and administrators".[29] However, knowing that it is an orchestrated and well-funded campaign doesn't help us understand why it has been taken so seriously, and has thus clearly resonated with vast swathes of the public. More importantly, it doesn't help us understand why liberal centrists and some leftists have jumped on the bandwagon with such enthusiasm. Nor does it help us understand the issues of substance that lie at its root, which despite the noise of the "scorching, end-is-nigh headlines" are real issues.[30]

One important answer, therefore, to why universities have become a key battleground in the renewed culture war is because they have been expressly targeted. There would be nothing necessarily wrong with think tanks trying to foster ideas and policies if they were open and transparent about doing so and were they not funded by organisations such as the Koch Foundation known to manipulate "democracy through dark money donations";[31] and were it not for the fact that in this case the campaign is so flagrantly hypocritical and contradictory.[32] The think tanks and media outlets pushing the free speech crisis narrative are doing some of the very things they are warning against. Free speech defenders claim to be concerned with open inquiry, the pursuit of truth, the neutral marketplace of ideas, and yet spreading propaganda, flooding the media with fear-mongering headlines and misrepresenting and insulting your opponents can hardly be said to help create the conditions for open and fair inquiry and the pursuit of knowledge. As Sleeper demonstrates, "The one thing threatening freedom of expression on campus is the 'free speech' crusade itself".[33]

Not that most journalists or politicians treat it as a crusade or as propaganda. Many are all too eager to believe the campaigners and often seem to take as fact claims that are evidently biased. One of the primary sources for many of the claims made about students is "The Coddling of the American Mind", a 2015 *Atlantic* article later expanded into a book, which can be considered the "manifesto"[34] or at least "best-known articulation" of the "free speech under threat" narrative. Its authors are Jonathan Haidt and Greg Lukianoff, the latter is the president of FIRE and as such, can hardly be deemed neutral. While Haidt, a self-identifying centrist, is cofounder of the Heterodox Academy, an advocacy group dedicated to disseminating the idea that there is a campus free speech crisis, that political correctness is running amok, and that there is a left-wing orthodoxy in universities stifling diversity of opinion. More importantly, their argument interprets recent student movements, campus controversies and general student behaviour through a particular and highly self-serving frame—speculative, pseudo-profound, self-help psychologising—and as such, is deeply depoliticising. The problem, they claim, is students' inability to toughen up because they have been weakened by pervasive "safetyism", a form of excessive protection of young people from real and imaginary dangers. Haidt and Lukianoff ignore political, economic and structural issues, arguing that "a campus culture devoted to policing speech and punishing speakers is likely to engender patterns of thought that are surprisingly similar to those long identified by cognitive behavioural therapists as causes of depression and anxiety". They therefore conclude that universities "should teach incoming students how to practice cognitive behavioural therapy".[35] If only students underwent CBT, they seem to suggest, then crippling debt or gross inequality or institutional racism or the lack of social justice or working forty-hour-plus weeks on minimum wage while studying would not be a concern to them; they could rise above it, happy in the knowledge that, despite all evidence to the contrary, establishment liberalism is managing things just fine and there is absolutely no need for any change whatsoever. In other words, they recognise that student mental health is a serious concern, but they blame the students themselves for this mental health crisis. It may be the case that CBT might help particular students experiencing particular problems, but as a blanket solution to deep-rooted social, economic and structural problems, and as an optic for analysing cultural phenomena, it is woefully inadequate, not least because it is a proposal to treat symptoms rather than causes.

DEBATE FETISH

A clear illustration of how successful the campus-free-speech-crisis campaign has been is the creation in the UK of a new higher education regulator—the Office for Students—that among other things will oversee free speech in universities. In October 2017, Jo Johnson, the then universities minister, announced that the Office for Students could "fine, suspend or deregister universities if they do not meet a statutory duty to commit to free speech in their governance documents". As a justification for this, Johnson said: "Our young people and students need to accept the legitimacy of healthy vigorous debate in which people can disagree with one another. That's how ideas get tested, prejudices exposed and society advances. Universities mustn't be places in which free speech is stifled". For, he continues, "free speech is one of the foundations on which our higher education tradition is built. It goes to the heart of our democratic values. . . . Our universities must open minds, not close them".[36]

Firstly, we should note that Johnson is expressing or rather parroting very conventional views on free speech and its relation to education and democracy. Such declarations are made ad nauseam. Indeed, his successor, Sam Gyimah, parroted the same views and even invented and exaggerated a few anecdotes for good measure.[37] Whether these views are true or not, or have any significant meaning, is rarely if ever questioned. The idea that freedom of speech is at the heart of democratic values is axiomatic.

So let's take a closer look at Johnson's statements. Firstly: "young people need to accept the legitimacy of healthy vigorous debate". Otherwise, the university will be punished. This statement is a typical piece of liberal chauvinism. *They* need to accept what *I* say is legitimate. And the implication is that young people should not challenge or question what he deems to be legitimate. He doesn't state that it is a matter of what he deems to be legitimate. It is legitimate. It is a given, even though in a great deal of cases it is precisely the question of legitimacy that is at stake. To have a debate there has to be a common point of departure, there has to be some stage-setting, points on which all participants agree. What recourse does one have if there is no common point of departure, or one fundamentally objects to the assumed common point of departure? That is not taken into consideration.

What about healthy vigorous debate? What exactly is it? Is it, for example, the kind of debating we see in the House of Commons? Overgrown schoolboys braying, hooting and howling while waving bits of white paper in the air; House of Commons' debates which feature pre-scripted questions and rote responses, if they are answered at all; the House of Commons, with its three-line whips; arcane and utterly undemocratic customs and rules. The pantomime absurdities of the House of Commons, however, illustrate a very important point about debate, which is that it is convention and rule-governed. Many of these conventions and rules are unwritten, but this invisibility only makes them all the more ideologically significant. These conventions and rules guide, fix and determine what it is possible to say and do within any given setting. In the House of Commons, there is very little free speech of the kind demanded by free speech absolutists (as is the case with most institutions). These conventions and rules are arbitrary and historical and came into existence because a particular group of people with a shared set of interests determined their value and usefulness. Overtime they came to be naturalised and normalised, such that they are seen to be not only the best but the only way to conduct debate.

But Johnson can't be blamed for the House of Commons, so maybe he means something else by vigorous healthy debate. Maybe he's thinking of the way debate takes place in universities. And before considering its health or vigour the first question we need to ask is whether debating does actually take place in universities, and if so, in what form. It is the case that universities feature different forms of ideas being exchanged—lectures, seminars, workshops. The events that seem to create headlines, however, are usually to do with guest speakers invited to give a lecture. So let's be clear; a lecture is not a debate. A lecture is someone given a platform to speak to an audience for a given amount of time. The speaker is introduced, usually in highly flattering terms (this is a convention), and the audience is invited to feel privileged that such a speaker is going to share important ideas with them. In other words, the very framing of the event establishes the value and validity of invited speakers and their ideas. The speaker then makes an argument or at least presents a set of ideas to the gathered audience. At the end of the lecture there may be a question and answer session. This, at a stretch, could be considered a debate. But even here, the chair of the event decides who gets to ask questions and the lecturer gets to choose whether or not to answer them. Lecturers therefore hold all the cards. They have the platform. They can refuse to answer questions; they can dismiss or ignore them; they can be highly selective in how they answer them. In short, there exists a whole range of options that ensure that whatever else takes place it will not be much of a debate. In other words, Q and A's are largely performative.

But let's assume debates do exist. What does it mean for a debate to be considered vigorous and healthy? Well, firstly, why this obsession with vigour? Here are some synonyms of vigorous: zealous, fervent, vehement, fiery, wild, unrestrained, uncontrolled, unbridled; tough, blunt, hard-hitting. Is this really how we want people to behave in a debate? It is certainly not how lecturers want their students to behave. Indeed, students are usually criticised by people like Johnson for being zealous and uncontrolled. The free speech brigade do want students to be tough and possibly hard-hitting, but why? Why are these qualities valorised? Is being blunt and hard-hitting the best way to arrive at truth? Or might it be a particular approach that benefits some groups of people more than others? Might this obsession with vigour be ideological?

This language of vigour, of being hard-hitting, 'wiping the floor with' and 'destroying' opponents is not only highly gendered but hyper-competitive, even militaristic. It is also a highly infantile conception of communication, but one that benefits people with structural power. It is to confuse critical thinking with winning an argument or making a legal case or being opinionated. This obsession with being tough and winning indicates that the people most invested in debate are those that most stand to benefit from it being one of the dominant forms of political discourse, and this is in part because the conditions of debate already confer advantage on certain kinds of speakers. Certain voices, faces and views are perceived to be authoritative, and others less so. This is not solely a question of those with significant positions of authority, such as judges, professors, doctors or news anchors, but also those with assumed authority, such as middle-class, middle-aged white men. One need merely think about the way white men in suits are treated compared to young men of colour dressed in casual wear. The latter frequently, indeed systemically, suffer what Miranda Fricker calls "epistemic injustice". Fricker argues that women and minority groups are often treated as lacking credibility. Because of a given hearer's prejudice about the social type to which a woman or ethnic minority belongs, their views, arguments or opinions are not believed or are easily dismissed; they suffer a credibility deficit. This form of injustice causes great harm. By not being taken seriously as a knower one is not being taken seriously as a human being. Among many other damaging effects, it can make one less willing to participate in debates, or to participate less fully.[38]

Finally, even if healthy vigorous debate does exist or is possible, is it the best way for decisions to be made, for policies to be decided, for truth to be pursued, for minds to be changed, for enlightenment, knowledge and understanding to be furthered? Most debates are confected and largely pre-scripted; they are theatre, and usually an opportunity for people to promote their ideas, not finesse them. Most academic disciplines do not rely on or use debate to further knowledge. Being tough and 'winning' debates do not display depth of understanding or a sophisticated level of engagement. What politicians such as Johnson and free speech warriors in general seem unable to countenance is that there might exist alternative modes of learning, that a constructive supportive environment might lead to deeper engagement with challenging material; that there might exist different, even better, modes of pursuing truth, practicing democracy and developing one's moral autonomy than barking soundbites or being 'controversial'—simple things such as collaborating, listening and being respectful; or interrogating and acknowledging one's privilege and prejudices.

SAFE SPACES

Many of the fears about free speech on campus concern what are perceived to be the latest student fads—safe spaces, no-platforming and trigger warnings—which are dismissed by free speech warriors because of their belief that discomfort, and challenging ideas and environments, are essential to learning. In the same interview cited above Johnson says, "No-platforming and safe spaces shouldn't be used to shut down legitimate free speech". In criticising them, Johnson and many others repeat the same assumptions about what universities are for and what constitutes learning and the acquirement of knowledge. Such claims are rarely substantiated. University, we hear, is for broadening one's mind, sharpening one's wits, having one's ideas challenged, being exposed to uncomfortable ideas and overcoming innate assumptions. And hence, it is argued, students need to be tough: "some discomfort is inevitable in classrooms if the goal is to expose students to new ideas, have them question beliefs they have taken for granted, grapple with ethical problems they have never considered, and, more generally, expand their horizons so as to become informed and responsible democratic citizens".[39] Such a generalising argument ignores the fact that different things might make students uncomfortable and that the differences might be highly significant. The discomfort caused by questioning someone's opinions or beliefs and that caused by questioning someone's humanity, dignity or validity are not the same thing. Racist or sexist speech will most likely be uncomfortable or scary to someone who may, with good reason, fear that it is a prelude to physical violence. It is not difficult to imagine such situations. Or a target of such speech "might feel threatened, objectified, or dehumanized . . . or reminded of their subordinate social status or their status as sex objects".[40]

We repeatedly hear that students are afraid of controversial ideas, and yet we are rarely told what exactly these ideas are. One suspects this is because "uncomfortable ideas" or "unpopular views" are often merely euphemisms for "racist" or "sexist" views, for retrograde claims that have already been challenged and discredited some time ago. We repeatedly hear that the best cure for bad ideas is to bring them into the open for discussion, an argument which, as we'll see in the next chapter, is based on faulty empirical assumptions. Furthermore, it ignores the fact that many of these so-called uncomfortable ideas have been discussed a great deal, and have been shown to be not only worthless but harmful, and harmful to all the things free speech defenders claim to hold dear—democracy, education, reason, truth. Racist claims for example are not philosophically considered thoughts worthy of engagement. To reply with reasoned speech to racist speech is potentially to confer legitimacy onto that speech.

Commentators argue that critical thinking is being diminished, and yet they are unable to see that student protests might be the result of thinking as much as feeling. And that students might not accept the reductive binary so beloved of liberal rationalists between thought and feeling—a binary that has deep roots in the Western philosophical tradition, and has served all sorts of oppressive purposes, such as dehumanising women and colonised subjects; a binary that has been discredited not only by the philosophical insights of feminism and thinkers such as Nietzsche, Marx and Freud, but also by contemporary psychology, behavioural economics and cognitive science.[41] The claim that it is mere feelings that motivate student protests or criticisms is dismissive and patronising in a manner typical of both patriarchal and colonialist reasoning—this is just their feelings, they are underdeveloped, or lack the mature use of reason that 'we' possess, and once they grow up they'll get over these petty and unrealistic demands for justice.

If there is one group of people who clearly struggle to question the beliefs they take for granted it is the liberal commentariat—a relatively homogeneous group of similarly educated people from shared class and cultural backgrounds, who repeatedly display their discomfort with new ideas and with ethical problems they've never considered. (One need only consider the issue of gender-neutral pronouns and the difficulty and discomfort, if not apoplectic rage, many people seem to experience when asked to address a person as they rather than he or she.)

Jeffrey Aaron Snyder writes that "without the stimulation to interrogate our basic assumptions or to consider alternatives to our preferred explanations, our own ideas will devolve into pathetic caricatures", and he is possibly right, but not in his target.[42] Free speech warriors rarely interrogate their basic assumptions, and thus their commonplace arguments often resemble pathetic caricatures. Many of the articles criticising campus politics demonstrate that it is liberal commentators who are entitled and mollycoddled, sensitive to criticism, and unwilling to debate (this will be examined in more detail in chapter 3). As Moira Weigel notes, they designate themselves the arbiters of which conversations or political demands deserve to be taken seriously and which do not; and they complain that other people are enforcing speech codes, while attempting to enforce their own.[43] The clearest example of this is successful, widely published establishment figures, "privileged, confident voices who have framed every debate since time immemorial",[44] attempting to paint themselves as beleaguered victims because their ability to indiscriminately offend, exclude, and dominate has been challenged; because, for example, they are no longer able to celebrate the achievements of British colonialism without being criticised for dubious scholarship.[45] "Pale, stale males are the last group it's OK to vilify", claims Simon Jenkins joining a chorus of 'down-trodden', 'silenced' men such as Stanford professor Niall Ferguson with his column in *The Sunday Times*, global celebrity Jordan Peterson and many other fatuous, predictable bores.[46] A better example of pathetic caricatures would be hard to find.[47] Other pale stale males include members of the so-called intellectual dark web—so dark most of them are selling out stadiums, reaching million-plus viewers on YouTube and regularly feature in legacy media outlets. The woe-is-me-the-poor-white-man narrative is an example of the common tactic of appropriating the rhetoric of victimhood and turning advantage into disadvantage by performing one's power as powerlessness. The cry of 'political correctness gone mad' or the accusation that students are totalitarian are what Anshuman Mondal describes as "forms of performativity that re-order power relations by rhetorically positioning dominant groups at a disadvantage in relation to minority groups".[48]

Unlike such conformist defenders of the status quo, many student protestors are doing exactly what some free speech advocates, such as J. S. Mill, claim free speech is for: they are asking for people in authority, in positions of power, such as the authors of free speech scare stories, to question their unexamined beliefs, to address power imbalances; they are seeking to "open up scholarly debate to a broader range of perspectives" and to advance social change;[49] they are attempting to reveal the ideological basis of white men's authority and to unveil "the university's exploitative practices and its deeply embedded structures of racism, sexism, and class inequality".[50] Student activists are precisely offering alternatives to preferred explanations and opening minds, not closing them. As Derecka Purcell notes, "reclaiming spaces, reshaping curricula, renaming buildings, and replacing school crests serve as means to spark debates, not as ends in themselves".[51]

No platforming, demanding safe spaces and other forms of disruptive politics draw attention to the structures underlying conventions, rules, practices and normative forms of politics. In particular, they question the privileging of certain practices such as debate, and they question the conditions of possibility of debate, who determines who gets a platform and why. By refusing to participate in or by protesting a given event, students are questioning and challenging the structure and context, as much as the content, of such an event and thus posing a much greater challenge to critical thinking than some two-bit self-promoting opportunist racist or transphobe spouting intentionally provocative nonsense.

What's more, safe spaces, trigger warnings and no platforming can all be viewed as supporting and extending free speech, not curtailing it. But they are supportive in a manner that establishment liberals disapprove of. Safe spaces allow for different voices to be heard and different kinds of discussion—the aim of safe spaces, argues Sara Ahmed, is precisely to "enable conversations about difficult issues to happen".[52] Students may be attempting, for example, to raise awareness of the ways in which white students occupy a normative position in seminars, and how this might involve an unacknowledged identification with white supremacist or colonialist attitudes if they inadvertently use homogenising terms to describe people of colonised cultures, for example. Confronting these unintentional identifications and their implicitly exclusionary effects on students who cannot occupy this normative position is what making seminars safe means, not filling the room with beanbags and only discussing 'comfortable' topics. Trigger warnings may allow for seminar groups to self-reflect on, analyse and interrogate the process of what they are doing and no platforming can be an expressive form of protest, an attempt to establish a different point of departure for debate than that contrived by established power structures. In many important ways, therefore, students are in fact being much truer to democracy in their attempt to critique institutions and structural power. As Jedediah Purdy notes, "Democracy has essentially been a norm-breaking political force wherever it has been strong. It has broken norms about who can speak in public, who can hold power, and which issues are even considered political".[53]

UNPREPARED FOR THE REAL WORLD

Students on campus are protesting and challenging different forms of oppression. But the commentariat argue that by wanting to inhabit a space without racism, sexism or transphobia, by refusing to engage with "uncomfortable" ideas, students will be unprepared for the real world. The assumption seems to be that the real world is racist, sexist and unjust, and students just need to accept this, or at least, challenge such injustices in a manner that liberals deem appropriate, even though there is ample evidence to show that such methods achieve very little. They are not wrong that the real world is full of injustice, violence and oppression, but the "real world" of their imaginary seems to be some bar of the Wild West and not the highly controlled, surveilled, policed, micromanaged world of twenty-first-century neoliberal capitalism. Does the average workplace, for example, not have strict codes of conduct and speech? How much free speech, let alone offensive speech, is there in the average workplace? All workplaces are governed by a set of implicit and explicit codes—many of which are much more draconian then even the most liberal of liberal arts colleges. The idea that the real world is this free-for-all, open and equal space of absolute free speech is a fantasy. More important, though, is the fact that students already inhabit the real world, not only in the sense in which their concerns are wider social and political ones and in which "universities are not walled off from the 'real world' but are corporate entities in their own right",[54] but also in the practical sense in which most students do paid work to support their studies, often in highly challenging real-world environments, possibly much 'realer' than the rarefied world of cosmopolitan journalists. If, however, the students being referred to are those that don't work in the real world, but belong to elite, privileged universities, then the problem might be privilege, elitism and entitlement, not students.

One very noticeable feature of the university free speech crisis narrative is how little media space is given to the voices and views of the subjects concerned—actual students. Students are silencing us, we hear from people on major media platforms; white men are under attack report white men in their major newspaper columns, major journal articles and network TV interviews, which then get cited and repeated ad nauseam. And yet students are not being heard. Students are not given mainstream media platforms, let alone on a weekly basis. Students are rarely given a right of reply. They are not given the opportunity to represent their own views and arguments. Who are these students, and is it really possible to generalise about such a massive and diverse cohort of people? Are they really a homogenous bunch of dupes, drinking cultural Marxist Kool-Aid, unable to think for themselves and emotionally fragile and sensitive? Rarely are student concerns considered legitimate, indeed they are rarely given any consideration at all. This is not engagement. Not only are their concerns not addressed or taken seriously, more often than not they are dismissed or trivialised, and the students themselves are subject to a vicious backlash.

The reality of student life is markedly different from the picture most commonly painted in dominant accounts, which, as Ana Mari Cauce notes, are "false in so many ways, and even insulting".[55] In *Kids These Days* Malcolm Harris provides a detailed account of the difference between student stereotypes and the reality of student life. Most students do not attend elite universities and will not obtain well-paid, secure jobs after graduation; most students have to work in low-paid jobs to subsidise their study and many work nights or long hours; many students are likely to experience food insecurity or periods of homelessness; and almost all students will incur massive debt.[56] Harris situates his account of student life in a broader narrative about the ravages of neoliberalism, arguing that it is millennials who bear the greatest brunt of it. Students today, shows Harris, have less control of their lives than ever before leading to increasing levels of anxiety, depression and other stress-related mental and physical illnesses.[57] But rather than address this, both politicians and the liberal commentariat prefer to pathologize students, and to blindly insist upon the importance of the values that their policies and ideology have utterly undermined. They profess to defend the university as a space of academic freedom and open inquiry able to help students develop moral autonomy and intellectual fulfilment and yet they have increasingly sought to transform university education into an instrument in the service of capital. Higher education, notes Wendy Brown, has been "reconfigured by neoliberal rationality as an investment by human capital in the enhancement of its own future value; this transformation makes literally unintelligible the idea and practice of education as a democratic public good".[58]

It is not unusual that in times of crisis the establishment will attempt to generate panic or alarm that can distract attention from their own role in both generating and mismanaging such a crisis. One possible reason why there is such an exaggerated focus on small-scale episodes of student politics is that it is a way of preventing a more widespread scrutiny of much bigger threats, not only to free speech but also to democracy, both on and off campus. As Will Davies argues,

> The suggestion that young people are uniquely intolerant and self-indulgent is a useful way of avoiding talking about other things. It throws the blame back on to a generation that is now suffering the aftermath of the credit-based economic model that, with a little help from monetary policy-makers, inflated their parents' house prices and pension pots. At a time when student mental health is deteriorating, the panic surrounding 'free speech' reinforces the notion that there is something wrong with young people, and not with their environment.[59]

It is worthwhile asking who has most power to stifle free speech. Is it students, using their increasingly curtailed, constrained and policed right to protest, or might it be university managers with the force of law on their side? University managers who can shut down venues, suspend or fire troublesome staff members; university managers who are increasingly involved in governing all aspects of university work, including course curricula; university managers who stage-manage empty consultation exercises and ride rough-shod over previously established agreements and standards, who frequently ignore the 'tough questions' they are so keen for students to cope with. What is more likely to stifle speech—student demands (that are necessarily the result of discussion and consensus as they involve a plurality of voices) or the marketisation of higher education and the fact that universities are now beholden to a raft of absurd metrics?

Schlosser argues that one reason professors or lecturers are scared of students is because they fear they might lose their jobs, which may occur if a student complains or gives a lecturer a bad rating. This is not an unreasonable fear. It is reasonable to be concerned about one's job security, especially in an increasingly insecure form of employment. But it is not reasonable to blame the lack of job security in the higher education sector on students. The fact that student evaluations play a significant role in determining whether contracts are renewed is not the fault of students; the fact that a majority of university staff are on zero-hour or fixed-term contracts is not the fault of students; the fact that the lecturer-student dynamic has shifted is not the fault of students. The fact that universities today are metrics-obsessed, ratings-chasing, consumer-led competitive organisations increasingly run like businesses is not the fault of, and is of little benefit to, students.[60] It is the fault of politicians, think tanks, university senior management groups and the wider environment of marketisation, neoliberalism and a ceaseless right-wing onslaught on the idea of the public university as a public good. As Sleeper argues, "If anything, the real threat to free inquiry isn't students, but that same market imperative that First Amendment defenders claim to hold dear. Most university leaders serve not politically correct pieties but pressures to satisfy student 'customers' and to avoid negative publicity, liability and losses in 'brand' or 'market share'".[61]

If students have been empowered it is free-market libertarians who have brought this about, but it is a highly circumscribed and illusory form of power: They are empowered as consumers and glorified survey-bots. The ideology promoted by free market libertarians has meant that provision is now customer or consumer-oriented, but this shift doesn't necessarily benefit the student because consumer logic transforms what education is for and how it is perceived. It also decreases rather than increases freedom, since the "more market-driven a university, the more restrictive it is of individual rights in education".[62] Surveys and evaluations, for example, benefit university management, not students. Constant survey-based evaluations are a central part of data-driven management strategy, which has been imported from commercial business. This transfer of private-sector logics and ideology into the education sector has led to "the replacement of an ethos of public service with the discipline of the market and outcomes-based external accountability", which puts greater emphasis on outcomes and their measurement using quantitative data, thereby "increasing levels of managerialism, bureaucracy, standardisation, assessment and performance review".[63] None of which can be shown to have benefitted students. It is not only that universities are increasingly subject to market logics and neoliberal rationality, but higher education has become an industry, and an increasingly profitable one.[64] Even the *Economist* recognises the danger of this:

> Today's universities are in danger of being turned from temples of learning, where scholars introduced their young disciples into the mysteries of their calling, into teaching factories run by number-obsessed managers and divided into two classes: brand-name academics who are always on some junket and part-time teachers who are desperately trying to finish their PhDs while making enough money teaching to keep body and soul together.[65]

There is a great deal to be concerned about in higher education, but rare is the headline or discussion concerning, for example, the damaging effects of marketisation on higher education or the student mental health crisis, directly linked to debt and other social and economic pressures.[66]

There is a crisis in higher education, but what is most likely to have caused this crisis? Small groups of students attempting to raise awareness against normative forms of injustice and daring to propose norms about how they wish to be treated, or years of underfunding, ceaseless ideological attacks, spiralling student debt, a radical transformation in financing, an ever-increasing commercialisation of universities and rampant casualisation? It is clear that these repeated attacks on students—this blinkered focus on one issue at the expense of many others—are part of an attempt on behalf of people with power to maintain that power, and to deflect attention away from the multiple ways in which they are making not just universities but society and the planet less safe, more unequal, and more divisive. Free speech is an effective tool for achieving this because free speech reinforces existing power structures; it benefits conservatism, right-wing organisations and right-wing ideology more generally, and, basically, always has.

NOTES

1. To see just how much average newspaper readers care about students and university matters, read almost any below-the-line comments on articles concerning campus free speech issues. Very little seems to make people angrier.

2. Brendan O'Neill, "From No Platform to Safe Space: A Crisis of Enlightenment", in *Unsafe Space: The Crisis of Free Speech on Campus*, ed. Tom Slater (London: Palgrave, 2016), 8.

3. For an amusing example of just how elite, consider the claim made by the *Times* that BBC chief political correspondent Laura Kuenssberg is an outsider, as she only went to Edinburgh and not Oxbridge. Janice Turner, "How Political Editor Laura Kuenssberg Broke the Mould to Become the BBC's Brexit Guru", *Times*, March 30, 2019.

4. Cited in Michael Roth, "Inequality and the 'Once and Future Liberal'", *Inside Higher Ed*, August 31, 2017, https://www.insidehighered.com/views/2017/08/31/reflection-mark-lillas-essay-and-book-about-identity-politics-essay.

5. Greg Lukianoff and Jonathan Haidt, "The Coddling of the American Mind", *Atlantic*, September 2015, https://www.theatlantic.com/magazine/archive/2015/09/the-coddling-of-the-american-mind/399356.

6. PEN America, *And Campus for All: Diversity, Inclusion and Freedom of Speech at U.S. Universities* (New York: PEN America, 2016), https://pen.org/wp-content/uploads/2017/06/PEN_campus_report_06.15.2017.pdf.

7. Kimberlé Crenshaw, "Race Liberalism and the Deradicalization of Racial Reform", *Harvard Law Review* 130 (2017): 2298.

8. Will Davies, "The Free Speech Panic: How the Right Concocted a Crisis", *Guardian*, July 26, 2018, https://www.theguardian.com/news/2018/jul/26/the-free-speech-panic-censorship-how-the-right-concocted-a-crisis.

9. Malcolm Harris, *Kids These Days: Human Capital and the Making of Millennials* (New York: Little Brown, 2018), chap. 2, Kindle.

10. Charles C. W. Cooke, "The New 'McCarthyism' Exists, but It Has Nothing to Do with Ted Cruz", *National Review*, March 25, 2015, http://www.nationalreview.com/article/415932/new-mccarthyism-exists-it-has-nothing-do-ted-cruz-charles-c-w-cooke.

11. Jonathan Haidt, "The Fragile Generation", *Spiked*, September 1, 2017, http://www.spiked-online.com/spiked-review/article/the-fragile-generation/20257#.

12. Edward Schlosser, "I'm a Liberal Professor, and my Liberal Students Terrify Me", *Vox*, June 3, 2015, https://www.vox.com/2015/6/3/8706323/college-professor-afraid.

13. Schlosser, "Liberal Professor".

14. Claire Fox, *"I Find That Offensive!"* (London: Biteback, 2016), 14, ebook.

15. Jeffrey Aaron Snyder, "Free Speech? Now, That's Offensive", *Inside Higher Ed*, September 1, 2016, https://www.insidehighered.com/views/2016/09/01/dangers-not-valuing-free-speech-campuses-essay.

16. Julian E. Zelizer and Morton Keller, "Is Free Speech Really Challenged on Campus?", *Atlantic*, September 15, 2017, https://www.theatlantic.com/education/archive/2017/09/students-free-speech-campus-protest.

17. For an excellent account of just how obsessed sections of the media are with this narrative check out the peerless *Citations Needed* podcast, "Episode 32: Attack of the PC College Kids!", https://citationsneeded.libsyn.com/episode-32-attack-of-the-pc-college-kids.

18. Tom Slater, "Introduction: Reinvigorating the Spirit of '64", in Slater, ed., *Unsafe Speech*, 2.

19. Mick Hume, *Trigger Warning: Is the Fear of Being Offensive Killing Free Speech?* (London: William Collins, 2015), 54.

20. Alberto Toscano, *Fanaticism* (London: Verso, 2017), 263.

21. Martin Mcquillan, "Gyimah's Freedom of Speech Claims under Scrutiny Again", *Research Professional*, June 29, 2018, https://www.researchresearch.com/news/article/?articleId=1375991.

22. Jon Gould, "Getting the Story Wrong on Campus Racism", *The Hill*, November 17, 2015, https://thehill.com/blogs/pundits-blog/education/260379-getting-the-story-wrong-on-campus-racism.

23. See Vimal Patel, "Yes, Students at Sarah Lawrence Are Demanding Free Detergent. But There's More to It Than You Might Think", *Chronicle of Higher Education*, March 15, 2019, https://www.chronicle.com/article/Yes-Students-at-Sarah/245913.

24. Eleanor Busby, "Claims Students Have Created University Free Speech Crisis Have Been 'Exaggerated', Says Report", *Independent*, March 27, 2018, https://www.

independent.co.uk/news/education/education-news/free-speech-students-uk-universities-human-rights-no-platforming-higher-education-a8276246.html.

25. Zack Beauchamp, "Data Shows a Surprising Campus Free Speech Problem: Left-Wingers Being Fired for Their Opinions", *Vox*, August 3, 2018. https://www.vox.com/policy-and-politics/2018/8/3/17644180/political-correctness-free-speech-liberal-data-georgetown.

26. PEN America, *And Campus for All*.

27. See for example, Davies, "Free Speech Panic"; Jim Sleeper, "The Conservatives behind the Campus 'Free Speech' Crusade", *American Prospect*, October 19, 2016, http://prospect.org/article/conservatives-behind-campus-'free-speech'-crusade; George Monbiot, "How US Billionaires Are Fuelling the Hard-Right Cause in Britain", *Guardian*, December 7, 2018, https://www.theguardian.com/commentisfree/2018/dec/07/us-billionaires-hard-right-britain-spiked-magazine-charles-david-koch-foundation.

28. Charles R. Lawrence III, Mari J. Matsuda, Kimberlé Williams Crenshaw, and Richard Delgado, "Introduction", in *Words That Wound: Critical Race Theory, Assaultive Speech, and the First Amendment*, ed. Mari J. Matsuda, Charles R. Lawrence III, Richard Delgado and Kimberlé Williams Crenshaw (London: Routledge, 1993), 50–53, ebook.

29. Sleeper, "The Conservatives".

30. Snyder, "Free Speech?"

31. Mike Small, "Revealed: US Oil Billionaire Charles Koch Funds UK Anti-Environment Spiked Network", *Desmog*, December 7, 2018, https://www.desmog.co.uk/2018/12/04/spiked-lm-dark-money-koch-brothers.

32. Monbiot, "How US Billionaires Are Fuelling".

33. Sleeper, "The Conservatives".

34. Jim Sleeper, "What the Campus 'Free Speech' Crusade Won't Say", *Alternet*, September 4, 2016, https://www.alternet.org/education/what-campus-free-speech-crusade-wont-say.

35. Lukianoff and Haidt, "Coddling". For a devastating critique of their argument, see Moira Weigel, "The *Coddling of the American Mind* Review—How Elite US Liberals Have Turned Rightwards", *Guardian*, September 20, 2018, https://www.theguardian.com/books/2018/sep/20/the-coddling-of-the-american-mind-review.

36. *Telegraph* Reporters, "Universities Told They 'Must Commit to Free Speech' under New Plans", *Telegraph*, October 19, 2017, http://www.telegraph.co.uk/news/2017/10/19/universities-told-must-commit-free-speech-new-plans.

37. Mcquillan, "Gyimah's Freedom of Speech".

38. See Miranda Fricker, *Epistemic Injustice: Power and the Ethics of Knowing* (Oxford: Oxford University Press, 2007).

39. American Association of University Professors, "On Trigger Warnings", August 2014, https://www.aaup.org/report/trigger-warnings.

40. Laura Beth Nielsen, "Power in Public: Reactions, Responses, and Resistance to Offensive Public Speech", in *Speech and Harm: Controversies over Free Speech*, ed. Ishani Maitra and Mary Kate McGowan (Oxford: Oxford University Press: 2012), 154.

41. Brian Leiter, "The Case against Free Speech", *Sydney Law Review*, 38, no. 407 (2016): 420–21. See also Christine Delphy, *Separate and Dominate* (London: Verso, 2012).

42. Snyder, "Free Speech?"

43. Moira Weigel, "Political Correctness: How the Right Invented a Phantom Enemy", *Guardian*, November 30, 2016, https://www.theguardian.com/news/audio/2016/dec/19/political-correctness-how-the-right-invented-a-phantom-enemy-podcast.

44. Afua Hirsch, "The Fantasy of 'Free Speech'", *Prospect Magazine*, February 16, 2018, https://www.prospectmagazine.co.uk/politics/the-fantasy-of-free-speech.

45. "Oxford Uni Don Says 'Peer Pressure' Is Stifling Debate", BBC, February 2, 2018. https://www.bbc.co.uk/news/uk-england-oxfordshire-42887083.

46. Simon Jenkins, "Pale Stale Males Are the Last Group It's OK to Vilify", *Guardian*, December 15, 2016, https://www.theguardian.com/commentisfree/2016/dec/15/pale-stale-males-blamed-brexit-trump.

47. Niall Ferguson, "Join My Nato or Watch Critical Thinking Die", *Sunday Times*, April 14, 2019, https://www.thetimes.co.uk/article/join-my-nato-or-watch-critical-thinking-die.

48. Anshuman A. Mondal, *Islam and Controversy: The Politics of Free Speech after Rushdie* (London: Palgrave Macmillan, 2014), 28.

49. Davies, "Free Speech Panic".

50. Robin D. G. Kelley, "Black Study, Black Struggle", *Boston Review*, March 7, 2016, http://bostonreview.net/forum/robin-d-g-kelley-black-study-black-struggle.

51. Derecka Purnell, "Black Study, Black Struggle": Forum Response", *Boston Review*, March 7, 2016,.

52. Sara Ahmed, "Against Students", *New Inquiry*, June 29, 2015, https://thenewinquiry.com/against-students.

53. Jedediah Purdy, "Normcore", *Dissent*, Summer 2018, https://www.dissentmagazine.org/article/normcore-trump-resistance-books-crisis-of-democracy.

54. Kelley, "Black Study".

55. Ana Mari Cauce, "Messy but Essential", *Inside Higher Ed*, November 20, 2017. https://www.insidehighered.com/views/2017/11/20/why-we-need-protect-free-speech-campuses-essay.

56. For an account of debt's devastating, though common effects see M. H. Miller, "The Inescapable Weight of My $100000 Student Debt", *Guardian*, August 21, 2018, https://www.theguardian.com/news/2018/aug/21/the-inescapable-weight-of-my-100000-student-debt.

57. Harris, *Kids These Days*, 4.

58. Wendy Brown, "Neoliberalism's Frankenstein: Authoritarian Freedom in Twenty-First Century 'Democracies'", *Critical Times* 1, no. 1 (2019): 62.

59. Davies, "Free Speech Panic".

60. Jerry Z. Muller, "The Tyranny of Metrics: The Quest to Quantify Everything Undermines Higher Education", *Chronicle of Higher Education*, January 21, 2018, https://www.chronicle.com/article/The-Tyranny-of-Metrics/242269.

61. Jim Sleeper, "Political Correctness and Its Real Enemies", *New York Times*, September 3, 2016, https://www.nytimes.com/2016/09/04/opinion/sunday/political-correctness-and-its-real-enemies.html.

62. Sleeper, "Conservatives".

63. Julia Evetts cited in Gary L. Anderson and Michael Ian Cohen, "The New Democratic Professional: Confronting Markets, Metric and Managerialism", https://www.unite4education.org/global-response/the-new-democratic-professional-confronting-markets-metrics-and-managerialism.

64. Raewyn Connell, "Ivory Tower and Market, The Silent Privatisation of Higher Education", Unite for Quality Education, August 22, 2018, https://www.unite4education.org/global-response/ivory-tower-market-the-silent-privatisation-of-higher-education.

65. Bagehot, "Some Thoughts on the Crisis of Liberalism—and How to Fix It", *Economist*, June 12, 2018, https://www.economist.com/bagehots-notebook/2018/06/12/some-thoughts-on-the-crisis-of-liberalism-and-how-to-fix-it.

66. The student mental health crisis is becoming increasingly serious. There has been a surge in students suffering from anxiety, depression and mental breakdowns, with suicide rates reaching alarming levels. See Samira Shackle, "'The Way Universities Are Run Is Making Us Ill': Inside the Student Mental Health Crisis", *Guardian*, September

27, 2019, https://www.theguardian.com/society/2019/sep/27/anxiety-mental-breakdowns-depression-uk-student.

Chapter Three

Racial Liberalism

The United States and the United Kingdom are structurally, institutionally, systemically racist, and racism pervades everyday life and language. The fact that this even needs to be stated, let alone explained, is itself testament to just how deep-rooted racism is. Racism operates in multiple ways. And one of the most powerful ways is through the denial that it exists, and through the denial that particular forms of behaviour or speech or structures are racist. The denial of racism can take many forms, the most common being the idea that we inhabit post-racial or colour-blind societies, an idea that relies on appeals to the seemingly contradictory but compatible notions of individualism and universalism—that is, to claims that we are all (different) individuals and that we are all human beings, and so the same.[1] The latter relies on what Kimberlé Crenshaw calls the "familiar and reassuringly non-racialised rhetorics of universalism [which] denies the continuing salience of racial power".[2] Both discourses "work to deny white privilege and the significance of race",[3] and both underpin common free speech arguments.

The conventional or common-sense account of racism is that it is a form of individual prejudice—an individual judging or treating another person or group of people negatively because of the colour of their skin or a supposedly shared cultural, religious or ethnic characteristic. Such forms of prejudice clearly exist, but they don't properly explain racism, and indeed can help foster the idea that racism operates on a level playing field: that a person of colour insulting a White person on account of race is somehow the same thing as a White person insulting a Black person because of race. That such a view of racism exists and is taken seriously reveals both the dominance of liberal thought and the enduring existence of entrenched racism (as well as the pig ignorance of White people). Liberalism would have us believe that we are all autonomous individuals free to act and speak as we please and all our achievements and failures are the result of nothing but talent and hard work, or the lack of it. And that history, culture, economics, social norms and structural power differentials are only partially and contingently relevant to both our ability to flourish and to suffer harm. This narrative is central to the fantasy of post-racialism, which Joshua Paul describes as "a discourse that erases the actuality of racialised stratification, denies the effects of racist discrimination and maintains [that] a generalised equality of opportunity characterises social life".[4] Such a fantasy presumes, among other things, that to tackle racism all we need to do is tackle racist people and racist ideology. Scholars on racism, however, have shown that racism is a great deal more complicated than this and that it encompasses "economic, political, social, and cultural structures, actions, and beliefs that systematize and perpetuate an unequal distribution of privileges, resources and power between white people and people of colour" that benefits whites and disadvantages people of colour overall and as a group.[5] As Charles W. Mills puts it, "Racism (or global white supremacy) is itself a political system, a particular power structure of formal or informal rule, socioeconomic privilege, and norms for the differential distribution of material wealth and opportunities, benefits and burdens, rights and duties".[6] Free speech, as commonly conceived, is one of these norms, and has to be viewed as part of, and having its roots in, this unnamed racist political system, what Mills calls "racial liberalism". The idea of racial liberalism draws our attention to the fact that liberalism is racialised as white, and so to the erasure, or whiting-out, of the "past of racial subordination that current, seemingly genuinely inclusive varieties of liberalism now seek to disown".[7] This chapter will explore some of these forms of erasure and whiting out that persist in liberal societies, not least in supposed free speech controversies.

The figure of the student in free speech controversies is curiously and suspiciously genderless, sexless and race-less. Who is this generic student? Are students really all the same? Are the think pieces that disparage or bemoan their protests even attempting to discuss all students? Might it be the case that many of the hot-takes on student snowflakes are in fact referring to a particular group of students but are too coy or worse to describe or identify them? Robin D. G. Kelley notes that the 2015–2016 protests that took place across almost ninety universities in the United States "were led largely by Black students, as well as coalitions made up of students of colour, queer folks, undocumented immigrants, and allied whites".[8] Yet you would not know this from mainstream media reports and commentary, which tend to generalise about and homogenise all students, and avoid the issue of race whenever they can, using euphemisms and other forms of misleading rhetorical tropes that have the effect of whitening out the substantive issues. Were the students to be identified in terms of their race, might a discerning reader start to question the authors' supposed neutrality and concern for free speech? Indeed, the reader might view the use of the free speech defence in such contexts as a convenient smokescreen hiding their defence of white privilege and attempt to "restore order at the cost of racial justice".[9] By not identifying the students concerned, or rather, by not foregrounding or even mentioning the significant racial issues, are the authors enacting the very kind of racist erasure that the students might have been protesting in the first place?

These questions are important because in many of the so-called campus free speech controversies the identity and political identification of the students concerned matters—indeed, as we have seen, identity in politics always matters, despite what the broad coalition of the anti-identity politics brigade claim. Many of the most high-profile cases, such as the Halloween costume controversy at Yale, Charles Murray at Middlebury and the Rhodes Must Fall campaign at Oxford, concern issues of race and racism, and involve students of colour attempting to make themselves and their points of view heard. This matters because all too often students of colour have not been and are not heard, their protests and demands are not taken seriously; they are dismissed or brutally cracked down upon—all too evident in the massive backlash examined in chapter 2. (This is of course not unique to students or to the current political climate. People of colour have always had to struggle against a powerful white political class and media that systematically lies, misrepresents and does gross injustice to Black calls for change and Black issues in general.) In the rare cases when students of colour's demands are reported often only one aspect will be examined, which itself is usually misrepresented, and often in a manner which ridicules and belittles them still further. But whatever the case, their protests or demands soon get drowned out in a sea of screaming liberals (screaming in a "learned and reasonable" manner) outraged that anyone should dare challenge their way of doing things—even sympathetic critics usually repeat a version of the patronising argument that 'your concerns need to be considered, but perhaps you could express them a bit more reasonably, let's talk things through so that I can persuade you that we are right and you are wrong, oh-misguided-young-people'.

So, for example, in a classic piece of 'yes-but' apologia for Empire, establishment liberal Will Hutton argues in response to the Rhodes Must Fall campaign that yes, "Cecil Rhodes was a racist, but you can't readily expunge him from history", and therefore his statue in Oxford should not be taken down. Why pulling down a statue equals expunging from history is not explained. Hutton does not engage with the way in which statues and other forms of memorials constitute an uncritical celebration of historical figures. He reduces the argument to a simplistic all-or-nothing binary of either someone is wiped from history or else things stay as they are, offering instead a nice fireside chat about some of the problems with colonialism. He argues that we need to understand Rhodes's importance for liberal democracy. Rhodes, he claims, was instrumental in laying the "liberal constitutional foundations" of South Africa and therefore played a crucial role in enabling South Africa to become a democratic force. Rather than engage with any of the students' arguments concerning the whitewashing of history or the role statues and memorials play in normalising racism or racial hierarchies, he argues that what is needed "is to understand the historical context—which requires an open mind, freedom of debate and unobstructed access to facts".[10] This sounds perfectly reasonable, but it implies that the campaigners don't have an open mind or value freedom. It also implies a highly simplistic version of history; history as "unobstructed access to the facts". It is hard to know what this means in practice, as if history is just facts, which exist somewhere in a pristine state just waiting to be discovered provided nothing gets in the way. The implication seems to be access to facts unobstructed by ideology or political bias, as if some people have an ideology and others, such as liberals like Hutton, don't, and nothing is more ideological than the denial that one is ideological.

Even when the liberal establishment does attempt to give students of colour a voice, the bias of their entrenched view is all too evident. A clear example of this can be seen in PEN America's free speech report, which claims to, and in part does, engage with students' voices and concerns. The introduction, which emphasises how the report will offer a "balanced view", states that

> students have asked whether free speech is being wielded as a political weapon to ward off efforts to make the campus more respectful of the rights and perspectives of minorities. They see free speech drawn as a shield to legitimize speech that is discriminatory and offensive. Some have argued that free speech is a prerogative of the privileged, used to buttress existing hierarchies of wealth and power. Some have gone so far as to justify censorship as the best solution to protect the vulnerable on campus. These attitudes risk giving free speech a bad name.[11]

Note that it is the students' *attitudes* that risk giving free speech a bad name, not the possibility that free speech is being wielded as a political weapon or legitimising offensive speech (which it is). There is no sense that the students might be right or that there might be some validity to their claims. And they are claims which, far from being churlish gestures of protest, have their roots in critical race theory and feminist philosophy of language, both of which have subjected free speech to decades of in-depth, sophisticated critique, in the process demonstrating that "free speech not only fails to correct the repression and abuse subjugated groups must face but often deepens their predicament".[12] But in the PEN report there is no space given to the depth and complexity of the students' arguments. Furthermore, the source for this summary of students' views is an article, written by an academic, that is deeply critical of students.

A similar pattern can be seen at work in press reports. Repeatedly we see the media responding to and criticising student reactions rather than the issue that provoked the reactions. And the voices typically heard in the mainstream media are those of the liberal establishment, almost always singing from the same hymn sheet. They set the terms of the debate and they provide the dominant accounts of the protests, typically claiming that they were some form of emotional outburst caused by hurt feelings, and very rarely that they were a considered response to structural racism and injustice. And when they describe these emotions they rarely examine why students feel strongly about a given issue, let alone the possibility that such emotions might be a valid and justified response, or that feelings and thought are not so easy to separate; that such an event might mark a breaking point for people who have been historically silenced, dismissed or subjected to oppressive structures and norms; and that reasoned debate or being reasonable, that is, acting according to the oppressor's diktats, has led nowhere. In many cases, the event that becomes a news story is merely the latest incident in what are often long-term, ongoing campaigns, in which students have engaged in all the ways free speech apologists argue they should, such as informed debate. For example, an issue such as student reactions to pro-Trump graffiti on Emory campus garners media attention, producing the typical reaction of condemning oversensitive snowflakes needlessly fretting about a harmless bit of free-speech-protected chalking. But the particular incident on Emory came after students of colour had been in conflict with their administration for over a year over what they saw as a lack of fair treatment in comparison with other groups on campus. An Emory student Isabelle Saldaña is quoted in the *New York Times* as saying, "It's less about the actual chalkings, this isn't something that's unique to Emory. This is a national conversation, even an international conversation, on the value of Black and Brown people".[13]

All too often, however, the specificities of each individual case get white-washed as the story goes from being one about racism to one about free speech—a shift that, as Bennett Carpenter notes, "is itself an expression of white supremacy".[14] This pattern can be seen repeatedly and in all sorts of contexts, not solely in campus politics, but in a variety of anti-racist campaigns; any attempt to challenge or critique not only explicit racism but also the normativity of whiteness becomes side-lined or subsumed into an abstract discussion of free speech or political correctness or some other diversionary topic. As Jelani Cobb argues, "The default for avoiding discussion of racism is to invoke a separate principle".[15] In case after case in which the issue of race is raised the discussion soon becomes reduced to a specious argument about the importance of debate, of free and open discussion, and the airing of supposedly difficult ideas or uncomfortable truths. Such discussions are not only a diversion from the actual issue, but they also illustrate white liberals' refusal and inability to recognise that the issue is one of structural, institutional and epistemic injustice. They are unable or unwilling to see this because challenges to normative racism are challenges to the epistemological assumptions underlying liberalism. Such avoidance is an illustration of both white supremacy and what Robin DiAngelo has termed "white fragility", the defensiveness of White people when confronted by their complicity in racist structures or patterns of behaviour.

CHARLES MURRAY

Take the Charles Murray controversy. A prestigious liberal arts university, Middlebury College, invites the renowned proponent of scientific racism to give a talk, a talk that will be introduced by the college president. Murray is the joint author of *The Bell Curve*, a reactionary, widely discredited book that attempts to give racist social Darwinism scientific legitimacy, and is well-known for being a provocateur, "with a long history of coming to college campuses to create turmoil and foment hatred".[16] (The liberal press describe him as 'controversial', an ambiguous, but largely positive term that connotes edginess or non-conformity; a term that is repeatedly celebrated and marketised by free speech advocates and aggrieved white men, who use it to mask and legitimise what are little more than retrograde, debunked and objectionable views.[17] This term, like many others, is part of an arsenal of obfuscatory or euphemistic rhetoric that is particularly pernicious and absurd when it comes to race. The common-place use of *racially charged* in place of *racist* being the most obvious example. Faculty and students take issue with this invitation, as they don't think a "flawed notion of 'free speech'" should allow "individuals in positions of power to spread racist pseudoscience in academic institutions, dehumanizing and subjugating people of colour and gender minorities".[18] They protest. Initially with letters and petitions. Both existing faculty members and 450 alumni write informed, well-argued, "reasonable" letters questioning the validity of such an invitation, expressing their concern that a "discredited ideologue" funded by a reactionary think tank, should be legitimised in this way.[19] The event went ahead regardless. It was protested, and at the end of the event, as a small group of protestors attempted to confront Murray, the protests turned violent and a faculty member accompanying him was injured. At this point, it becomes a huge news story and one of the go-to examples about the chilling of free speech and for all future denigrations of snowflake social-justice-warriors.

The injured faculty member, Allison Stanger, is given a platform in the *New York Times* op-ed pages to explain what happened, to defend Murray's views and to criticise the students. She writes

> For us to engage with one another as fellow human beings—even on issues where we passionately disagree—we need reason, not just emotions. Middlebury students could have learned from identifying flawed

assumptions or logical shortcomings in Dr. Murray's arguments. They could have challenged him in the Q. and A. If the ways in which his misinterpreted ideas have been weaponized precluded hearing him out, students also had the option of protesting outside, walking out of the talk or simply refusing to attend.[20]

This boilerplate free speech argument misses the point of the protests and demonstrates a highly limited or non-existent understanding of racism (not surprising given that she claims Murray can't be racist because he married an Asian woman).[21] Yes, a racist talk can be a learning opportunity, but this is not a legitimate defence; indeed, it suggests that racist subject matter or subject matter from a racist is as good a learning resource as any other. It ignores the fact that content matters. There are other ways of learning about logical shortcomings than having to listen to a racist. More importantly, logic is irrelevant. One needs only a basic grasp of US history to know that arguments linking racial intelligence to persistent poverty are ideological distractions from more important issues, such as a history of systemic, structural discrimination.[22] There is even less support for such claims from a scientific basis, since there is now a clear consensus among scientists that race is a meaningless scientific category; that, for example, there is no genetic basis for claims about shared racial characteristics.

There's nothing challenging about having to revisit arguments that were won decades ago or having to prove one's equality or the validity of one's existence. Not only is it not challenging, it is positively harmful. As David Gillborn shows, "so-called 'debates' about race and IQ can do nothing but harm to Black students: no matter how often the pseudoscience is debunked, the argument provides new fodder for those who wish to explain race inequality by looking anywhere except at the actions and beliefs of White people". Fodder which has real and direct impacts on policy, and therefore on Black people's lives. And there is no harm done to White people who nonetheless insist on the importance of free speech and their right to speculate about minority groups on the basis of pseudo-science legitimised because of whiteness. Gillborn writes, "Under the guise of 'free speech', White people are free to engage in speculation about the nature of intelligence, without risk to themselves, in a situation where the costs are borne entirely by minoritized groups".[23]

Despite arguing about the importance of critical engagement, Stanger's article illustrates her own refusal to engage. She assumes that

Murray was prevented from being heard because his "misinterpreted ideas have been weaponised", thereby dismissing both faculty and student reactions to his invitation, and paying no attention to the fact that his ideas have indeed been weaponised, though not by student protestors but white supremacists and their enablers in mainstream political discourse. That's a key reason for the objections to Charles Murray; how his ideas have been used. Racial pseudoscience has been marshalled in all sorts of pernicious ways not only to misrepresent Black and other minority cultures, but to enact harmful and devastating policies. And it is part of a broader set of discourses that, argues Keeanga-Yamahtta Taylor, seek to explain Black inequality by blaming "Black people for their own oppression", thereby transforming "material causes into subjective causes" where the "problem is not racial discrimination in the workplace or residential segregation: it is Black irresponsibility, erroneous social mores, and general bad behaviour".[24] To make a case in defence of Murray is therefore to legitimise and normalise speculative race talk, which, as Gillborn notes, "is part of a wider network of beliefs and practices that has real-world impacts on the educational and life chances of minoritised groups in general, and Black people in particular".[25] The protests against Murray should not be viewed as merely a matter of campus politics addressing a long-forgotten controversy, and not only because *The Bell Curve* has "cast a shadow over the politics of race and science ever since" its publication.[26] Race science is on the rise and is increasingly being used to legitimise far-right ideology, but it is often being peddled by seemingly 'respectable' academics aiming to shape public debates around race and immigration, and make certain views acceptable.[27]

Media commentators and academics such as Stanger suggest that racist arguments simply need to be confronted with sound, reasoned arguments. For example Vice-Chancellor of Oxford University, Louise Richardson, says students need to "appreciate the value of engaging with ideas they find objectionable, trying through reason to change another's mind, while always being open to changing their own".[28] But this is to misunderstand and underestimate how discourse and racism function, and to overestimate the power of reason. Rhetoric, persuasion, propaganda and narratives as well as visual representations are much more significant than rational, reasoned argument for spreading and legitimising racism and any other form of prejudice. There's nothing rational or reasonable about being a racist or about racist speech—as Patrick Wolfe notes, racism "exceeds rational calculation", and citing Arendt, "has survived libraries of refutation".[29] This is in part because, as Delgado and Stefancic show, "the dominant pictures, images, narratives, plots, roles, and stories ascribed to, and constituting, the public perception of minorities are always dominantly negative".[30] Most racist speech uses all sorts of figurative tropes to wield its power and achieve its effects, and therefore, "no account of race that fails to address its emotive virulence can be adequate".[31] Racism is ideological not logical, and it is an ideology that has its roots in practice. Racism is not merely discursive; it is very real, with brutal consequences. Racism is not just the categorisation, but the treatment of groups of people as inferior, with all the horrifying aspects that this involves, from slavery to lynching, mass murder to mass incarceration. The idea that racism can be defeated with 'more speech' is a misguided delusion proposed by commentators dazzled by an ideal conception of speech practice. Though it might be the case that, as Joshua Cohen claims, "people have the capacity to change their minds when they hear reasons presented, and sometimes they exercise that capacity", this line of argument is "not responsive to the dangers associated with speech, which is that most of the time people are not reasonably persuaded of what is true, just, fair, or decent".[32] As such, argues Brian Leiter, "'More speech' is only a remedy for (some) bad speech in a world in which people usually, not merely 'sometimes', exercise the capacity of changing their views in response to reasons. That is not our world".[33] Furthermore, not only is there no evidence to show one can defeat racism with reason, there is little evidence to show that it can be done through linguistic means at all. The belief that ennobling narratives enlarge our sympathies and thus can help overcome racism, that we can "think, talk, read, and write our way out of bigotry and narrow-mindedness" is what Delgado and Stefancic call "the empathic fallacy", a self-serving liberal delusion that racism can be addressed without the need for profound systemic, structural and institutional change.[34] In addition to this, there is little evidence for the cherished 'best disinfectant is sunlight' theory: that the more racist hate speech is heard in public the more the public will turn away from it. As a recent report shows, far-right figures known for using free speech to defend their hate-fuelled attitudes and politics have seen tremendous growth to their personal brand—in terms of social media followers, financial support and media exposure.[35] Bringing racist speech into the sunlight is just as likely to make it grow as make it wither. The important issue for the normalisation of racist speech is the wider social, economic, cultural and political context, which abstract discussions of principle ignore.

Contrary to the dominant narrative that paints the students as mindless thugs, the Middlebury protestors in fact had eloquent, thoughtful and considered reasons for protesting. Elizabeth Siyuan Lee, for example, is quoted (though not given her own op-ed) in the *New York Times* as saying that,

> the format of Murray's talk did not allow for equal discussion. Were students, especially students of colour, expected to just sit and listen for 45 minutes to an individual who has written that they are inferior to whites? Do Asians have to accept Murray's assertions that we have "higher IQ's" than other races, and as a result become the metaphorical "punching bag" for issues surrounding race and class? Where was the avenue to speak out against such ideas? How could students engage in debate on an equal playing field when Mr. Murray had a stage and a microphone, and we were just members of the audience? Without a platform for legitimate discussion, it seems that students had few non-disruptive tools to get their voices heard.[36]

The Middlebury students recognised that when it comes to racist pseudoscience there is no "both sides of the debate" or "robust exchange of views"; they demonstrated their appreciation of the importance of intellectual inquiry and academic freedom, and yet their concerns and arguments were disregarded and dismissed not only by the mainstream press but by a group of Middlebury faculty members in a letter that appeals to supposedly 'unassailable' core principles to make their argument in defence of free speech. Their principles included the highly question-begging claim that "genuine higher learning is possible only where free, reasoned, and civil speech and discussion are respected" and the dubious claim that "only through the contest of clashing viewpoints do we have any hope of replacing mere opinion with knowledge".[37] This letter, published in the *Wall Street Journal*, unlike the students' carefully crafted point-by-point rebuttal,[38] and its appeal to a dogmatic list of unassailable principles points not only to the way mainstream free speech arguments suffer the fate Mill warned against—"the fate of degenerating into 'dead dogma'"[39] —but also to a deeper contradiction of free speech arguments, which is that there are necessary limits to free speech, and these depend on one's political position. Repeatedly we hear arguments about the need to say the unsayable, to push boundaries, for speech to be unfettered, and yet the promoters of the unsayable have their own set of unsayable and unthinkable things. For example, there is no sense that an alternative to liberal democracy or to a capitalist mode of production is even possible. They rarely if ever question basic liberal values and assumptions, or the basic tenets of capitalism. And yet it is precisely such things that people with a different approach to free speech seek to challenge, they seek to police certain speech norms precisely in order to challenge deeper ones.

Stanger and others are quick to condemn physical violence but pay no heed to structural violence or institutionalised sanctioned violence. Such a focus on individual acts of violence at the expense of much greater structural violence is highly ideological, as the former is used to deflect attention away from the latter.[40] This is a prominent trope in the way in which the media supports racial capitalism and neo-colonialism. It is not only that all and any acts of Black violence are roundly condemned and weaponised to perpetrate moral panics, and myths and stereotypes of the violent Black man, whereas acts of White violence are usually explained as the result of mental illness or bad apples, and in no way a reflection of whiteness. It is also that the underlying structural causes of Black violence are disavowed. Cultural or psychological explanations, such as canards about absent fathers, might be offered, eagerly and repeatedly regurgitated by politicians and the press, which further essentialise and demonise Black communities, but there will be little scrutiny of the structural or institutional ways, in terms of housing, education or employment, for example, in which people of colour are not only disadvantaged but subject to persistent injustice. This is one of the ways such apparent controversies perform ideological work, as they tend to focus on the individuals involved rather than on the institutions or structures, which are the primary and more significant objects of critique. The problem is not only Charles Murray's ideas but the institutional legitimisation of such things. The problem is with institutions and structures that display blithe indifference to calls for change and not only fail to address systemic inequality and injustice, but further entrench and normalise them.

But liberals such as Stanger don't or can't or won't engage on this level or with these arguments because they refuse to concede or even consider that many if not all of their cherished ideals—the foundations of liberalism—are racial constructs; are foundational not only to liberalism but to white supremacy. There is no acknowledgement of the structures of power that determine liberal democracies—which in this context means some people have the power to dictate the terms of discussion and others can only attempt to challenge them, but in the broader context means that whiteness is not only normative, but structurally violent. The Charles Murray event, and the standard arguments offered in its defence, demonstrate how little these establishment figures can understand, let alone tolerate, others attempting to challenge the terms of debate or how a given space is to be used or who deserves a platform to speak. It illustrates how any genuine challenges to normative orders are met with a blanket refusal to engage, or stonewalling. No wonder that sometimes people might react violently, for as Joan Scott notes, "Sometimes it requires extraordinary actions to make one's voice heard in a conversation that routinely ignores it".[41]

Aside from Stanger's rote repetition of the standard liberal arguments in defence of free speech, what also needs to be recognised is the significance of her being given such a high-profile platform to present her account, which white establishment liberals almost always are, where they assume the mantel of free speech martyrs, portray themselves as victims, insist on their right to be heard and rebrand racist ideas as illustrative of the sanctity of free speech. Rare is the occasion when protestors or students are given op-eds in the *New York Times*. And yet white liberals and their chorus of defenders claim the contrary, that they are the ones being silenced and that this undermines democratic values. It does not seem to occur to them that democracy, freedom and free speech might be undermined in a much more profound and damaging way by endemic structural racism; that social, political and economic inequality, injustice and pervasive forms of oppression are deeply anti-democratic, betray the much-vaunted liberal values of equality and inclusivity, and make freedom and democracy little more than ideological myths, serving only 'the people who count'.

In cases such as this, in which racist speech or a racist speaker is being defended, there is a double and seemingly contradictory logic at work. On the one hand, the actual offensive speech—that is, the content—gets bleached out and repackaged as 'controversial' and so potentially valorised as some kind of non-conformist, progressive form of critique of the powerful. But at the same time, racism more generally gets increasing amounts of airtime and publicity, and slowly certain harmful modes of speaking become normalised. As Will Davies notes, "The perennial irony of all free speech controversies is how much attention they end up bestowing on apparently censored and dangerous views".[42]

The Middlebury protests also illustrate how for free speech defenders and liberal centrists more generally protesting against racism is considered to be worse than the initial act of racism (just as people protesting police violence are often portrayed in the media as rampaging lawless criminals and the police as innocent keepers of the peace, and property damage is viewed as worse than state violence. This narrative is all too common in reports on protests involving people of colour: disproportionate focus on the violence, even when it is carried out by a tiny minority of otherwise peaceful and legitimate protestors; and side-lining of the actual issue—systemic and often deadly police brutality).[43] The racism is viewed as an example of free speech, whereas the protests as chillingly authoritarian, as ill-conceived emotional over-reactions by over-sensitive troublemakers incapable of seeing the advantages of living in a society that values equality as a principle, even if not in practice. Thus, without any hint of irony Richard Cohen writes about controversial speakers such as Murray that "far more dangerous than what any of these speakers has to say is the reaction to it".[44] Liberal centrists not only see individual anti-racist protests as more dangerous than acts of racism because of the way in which such protests are carried out, they also think that anti-racism itself is a problem. Figures such as Mark Lilla or Eric Kaufman argue that what they call "'anti-white radicalism' is a bigger problem than actual racial discrimination",[45] and such narratives can be seen to potentially have very real-world consequences such as legitimising the FBI's targeting so-called Black identity extremists.[46]

In some cases, such an inverted account of actually existing power dynamics is taken to absurd lengths. For example, Danielle Allen likens Charles Murray to the Little Rock Nine, arguing that he is a hero who displayed courage and fortitude in the face of the protests against him, which she criticises for being anti-democratic. After praising Murray, she proceeds to provide the staple free speech argument about defeating bad ideas with good ones, the importance of debate, civility and reasoned critique. "Rather than shouting down Murray", she writes, "the protesters should have read his work and figured out how to critique it".[47] Allen does not consider why students chose to protest in the way they did and does not consider that they may well have already read and critiqued Murray's work and thereby reached, through rational, reasonable deliberation and debate, the conclusion that his ideas did not merit a platform.[48] As it happens, students debated Murray's appearance for many days prior to the event. Neither does Allen consider that granting a platform to such a person with such ideas is tantamount to conferring legitimacy on him and them, and so further legitimising and normalising ideas that contribute to an already deeply hostile and violent environment for people of colour.

When (white) public figures such as Charles Murray experience the threat of violence, the commentariat are outraged, leaping to their defence. People of colour are routinely and increasingly subject to the threat of and actual violence and little anguish is expressed about this in the mainstream media. Studies show that hate crimes and hate incidents are on the rise, on campuses and in society at large, and yet this receives little attention from concerned commentators. It is important to note the lack of liberal hand-wringing over hate crimes and other expressions of hatred and prejudice, especially when seen in relation to the excessive airtime and column inches given to hand-wringing over protests against assaultive speech. As we've seen, propaganda is a question of emphasis, of what stories and events are given prominence and become talking points, and therefore get marshalled for political purposes. Though major events such as the tragic murder of fifty Muslims in Christchurch generate an outpouring of liberal condemnation of "maniac" far-right terror, there is far less attention paid to pervasive low-level racism, Islamophobia, xenophobia and anti-immigrant rhetoric so common in contemporary society, let alone any self-examination of the media's significant contribution to this environment.

HATE SPEECH

This speaks to a wider problem with free speech protection, which often means that more is done to protect assaultive speech and people who spread race hatred than the people subject to it, and so the negative effects come not "only from the hate message itself, but also from the government response of tolerance".[49] Often the very act of defending the right to speak itself does political work for what is said. It creates publicity, it makes the speech act an issue of debate and it can legitimise the content. Not only does free speech principle and law empower the powerful but it harms the less powerful. In the United States, for example, First Amendment law protects racists, but not victims of race hate speech. In examining case history Laura Beth Nielsen shows that "what happens in fact is that speech which targets people of higher social status is successfully regulated, and speech that targets people on the basis of their race and/or gender is struck down". She therefore comes to the "perhaps simplistic, but factually accurate" conclusion that "the law protects people from harassment and annoyance only when they are of a certain social status". It favours the powerful, and is hostile to the claims of people of colour.[50] This unequal treatment is made possible and is both legitimised and obscured by the theoretical underpinnings of racial liberalism.

To make matters worse, not only are people of colour not protected but the onus is on them to learn how better to deal with hate speech. Nielsen writes, "the law protects the powerful from harassment in public places while placing on its less privileged members an unrealistic duty to respond or accept their own subordination".[51] Free speech defenders make similar demands. For example, Timothy Garton Ash argues that the problem with "hate speech laws is that they tend to encourage people to take offence rather than learn to live with it, ignore it or deal with it by speaking back" and so his proposal, one thoughtlessly repeated by liberals, is that people "learn how to be a little more thick-skinned".[52] Such trite advice, amateur psychologising and indifference to people's suffering is testament to the chauvinism at the heart of many liberal free speech defences, and ignores not only structural issues, but performatively displays the dominance of liberalism and whiteness through the very insouciance with which issues of power are dismissed.[53] It also ignores the fact that hate speech is antithetical to the underlying liberal democratic principles that inform, among other things, Mill's arguments in *On Liberty* concerning the necessary background conditions for meaningful free speech to take place. Racist hate speech cannot be said to meet any of the criteria that determine the value of free speech; it doesn't enable the pursuit of truth, democratic deliberation or further moral and personal autonomy. Furthermore, there is a great deal of evidence to show not only that speaking back is far from straightforward, but that it doesn't work, not least because the intent and impact of racist speech is to end discussion, not to start or continue it.

Garton Ash's argument is also highly presumptive: Can hate speech simply be ignored, and are victims of it really less thick-skinned than establishment liberal white men? It is much more likely that people subject to hate speech are more thick-skinned, as they have had to experience offensive speech and worse for much of their lives. Whereas white male liberals' "apparent equanimity to all forms of offensiveness is a function of their power" and not their thick skin or open-mindedness.[54] On the contrary, as Robin DiAngelo shows, White people tend to be incredibly thin-skinned, especially when it comes to having their structural advantage brought to light, for if there is one thing white people find offensive it is being called white.[55] White people, especially straight white men, bristle or even become enraged at being called white. This is not because the term can be considered offensive—words and expressions that attempt to mock white people, and there aren't many of them, are not racist and pack no offensive punch.[56] It enrages them in part because they are deeply invested in thinking of themselves as individuals inhabiting a universal marketplace free of power differentials, but also because it racialises them, something they are not used to. And by doing so, it forces them to acknowledge that race is a social construct, one that confers privilege on them.

In *White Fragility* DiAngelo explores the racism underlying White people's problem with whiteness. White people, she argues, are used to be being in the dominant position, and so are almost always racially comfortable and have developed unchallenged expectations to remain so. They have not had to build tolerance for racial discomfort and thus "when racial discomfort arises, whites typically respond as if something is 'wrong' and blame the person or event that triggered the discomfort (usually a person of colour)".[57] This defensiveness is partly because "acknowledging racism as a system of privilege conferred on whites challenges claims to universalism".[58] And this is in part why many White people are so wedded to free speech and why free speech is so successful for marshalling aggrieved whiteness—it obscures this privilege and embodies the universal, a world of free individuals participating in the free marketplace of ideas. People defending the right to free speech in racial contexts or on racial matters are doing little more than defending the existing social and political order, and their place within the hierarchy. They are defending the liberal establishment's profound investment in whiteness. What many free speech controversies demonstrate is that self-declared liberals choose white privilege over racial equality every time; they choose their freedom over the freedom of oppressed others.

Garton Ash's argument, if you can call it that, is just one illustration of the way the free speech defence in practice works to amplify racist voices in the public sphere—racists should be allowed to keep speaking, while people of colour are expected to speak back or ignore racist speech and live with it. It also illustrates, and is in part based on, a limited understanding of both harm and power. In this respect liberals such as Garton Ash are in line with libertarians, as both tend to view harm in purely psychological terms due to their ideological investment in viewing freedom as located in the personal and private rather than the structural or economic. This in turn prevents them from acknowledging power asymmetries and the way in which racist speech acts are a form of power. The fact that liberalism disavows power relations, which it does through presenting itself in universal terms, does not mean that they don't exist in liberal societies. The disavowal is central to free speech arguments, but it is little more than a discursive trick. Liberalism, argues Mondal,

> perpetrates a rhetorical sleight of hand through an insistent series of abstractions that ignores the power relations within social life and thus fundamentally severs contemporary liberal arguments for freedom of speech from the world. Nowhere is this more apparent than in the conceptualization of speech as something distinct from 'action' because it does not have 'consequences'—which, in turn, means that speech does not matter.[59]

SPEECH ACTS

For the most part, free speech warriors take language for granted. They presume that language is a transparent window onto our thoughts, and that language is fundamentally descriptive. This reductive and traditional view of language and how it works is summarised in the banal idea that language is 'only words'. In *Trigger Warnings* Mick Hume argues that: "The first thing that seems to have been forgotten about free speech is that it's supposed to be Free. The second thing that is often forgotten is that it's simply Speech". He presumes that both freedom and speech are self-evident, and about speech he continues: "It is simply words. Words can be powerful tools, but there are no magic words—not even Abracadabra—that in themselves can change reality. Words are not deeds".[60] His associate Clare Fox makes a similar claim, confessing that when she gives talks on free speech to students she tells them that her "advice [is] that 'sticks and stones might break your bones, but words will never hurt me'".[61] That's right; she cites a nursery rhyme.

Hume and Fox belong to the *Spiked* collective, they are self-identifying free speech absolutists and campaigners, obsessed with snowflake students, and triggering the libs. They claim to be interested in intellectual progress and challenging conventions, but seem to have paid no serious attention to any of the significant intellectual developments of the last century. Their texts rely on and continually refer to the thinking of Milton, Locke and Mill. Brendan O'Neill, their fearless leader, acknowledges that there has been a "rethinking of the idea of the individual himself and his ability to exercise moral agency and judgement in the public sphere of discussion", but he does not attempt to explain let alone engage with the philosophical, theoretical or political reasons for this. He writes, "The old Millian view of the robust individual began to wither" as if it were some kind of organic process, and not the result of sustained critique from multiple academic disciplines, and therefore a sign of intellectual progress. He simply asserts the cartoonish claim that "we've seen the emergence of a view of the individual as 'acted upon' by speech, traumatised by ideas and lacking the firmness even to be able to read a book without therapeutic guidance".[62]

Their claims about language and speech are made without any supporting evidence. They casually dismiss the idea that words wound. O'Neill perfunctorily dismisses Richard Delgado's account of the ways in which words harm, calling it a dispiriting view, but without providing any counter-arguments or counter-evidence.[63] Assertion suffices. He holds his truths to be self-evident. This is unsurprising because the idea that words are simple or that they can't cause harm or are not deeds is risible, the stuff of nursery rhymes, and easily countered by even a cursory understanding of the philosophy of language or First Amendment jurisprudence. Starting with the most straightforward point, it is a matter of empirical fact that all sorts of actions—flag-burning or graffiti for example—that cannot be considered speech in the ordinary sense of the word are treated as speech and fall within the scope of a free speech principle, and likewise there are types of speech—speech used in the commission of verbal crimes, such as criminal solicitation or criminal conspiracy—that don't fall within the scope of a free speech principle. Therefore, shows Ishani Maitra and Mary Kate McGowan, "what counts as speech for the purposes of a principle of free speech is far more complicated than initially supposed".[64]

Secondly, the relation between speech and action is far less clear-cut than commonly assumed. Speech makes things happen in the world. Speech is performative. The philosopher J. L. Austin drew attention to the significant fact that in certain circumstances speakers perform acts merely by the words that they utter. Examples are things such as betting, marrying, christening, hiring, firing. These speech acts constitute an action; they bring about a change in the world. Furthermore, showed Austin, even in most ordinary cases where we use language, we often do or achieve something through it. Likewise, all sorts of actions constitute speech. This is not the view of liberal centrists' favourite straw man—the postmodern cultural Marxist—but Anglo-American analytic philosophy, social psychology as well as a raft of other academic disciplines, including linguistics, law and sociology. It is not merely, however, that speech performs actions, and that actions can be speech, it is that, as Wittgenstein demonstrated, language is a way or form of life, which is to say that language is embedded in, and for the most part inseparable from, our activities and practices. The consequences of this are far-reaching, not least for the law and First Amendment jurisprudence, for as Frederick Schauer shows "although some kind of free-speech-relevant distinction between speech and action is . . . a necessary condition for a meaningful free speech principle, it is by no means clear that such a distinction can be maintained".[65]

Thirdly, philosophers of language from Wittgenstein to Austin, Langton to Tirrell have shown that language is constitutive of reality rather than a reflection or description of it, that speech has the power to shape social being, that it works to normalise and secure certain beings and exclude and denigrate others, and therefore that significant speech acts are rarely free from questions of power. And if speech is never free of power, then liberal free speech arguments, which disavow power, need to be radically reconceived. This is far from an abstract or academic matter. On the contrary, as Lynne Tirrell shows in her analysis of the role of derogatory speech in the Rwandan genocide, linguistic violence is all too real and consequential. She shows that "derogatory terms, in use, engender actions creating and enforcing hierarchy" and that speech has the power "to facilitate the growth of both linguistic and broader social norms that make murder and mayhem come to be accepted".[66]

Finally, there is extensive empirical evidence that shows that speech doesn't merely lead to harm but itself causes and constitutes harm, both psychological and physical. As Mackinnon notes, "the powerful documentation of 'stereotype threat' in psychology shows an unquestionable harm done by racist speech".[67] Mari J. Matsuda writes, "The negative effects of hate messages are real and immediate for the victims. Victims of vicious hate propaganda experience physiological symptoms and emotional distress ranging from fear in the gut to rapid pulse rate and difficulty in breathing, nightmares, post-traumatic stress disorder, hypertension, psychosis, and suicide".[68] This harm should concern anyone who believes in liberal democratic principles, not least free speech, since victims of hate speech "are restricted in their personal freedom". Matsuda writes that "to avoid receiving hate messages, victims have to quit jobs, forgo education, leave their homes, avoid certain public places, curtail their own exercise of speech rights, and otherwise modify their behaviour and demeanour".[69]

It is crucial to recognise that speech harms not only individuals but entire groups, as assaultive speech significantly contributes to forms of exclusion and subordination. Indeed, according to Rae Langton, speech not only causes but constitutes subordination. Using Austin's conception of speech acts and performative language, she shows that "speech can constitute subordination by constituting norms that help to construct social reality for the subordinated group, norms which determine, first, the (relative) social status of the subordinated group; second, what rights and powers members of the group possess; and third, what counts as acceptable behaviour towards those members".[70] In other words, the problem with assaultive speech is not mere psychological discomfort, or a feeling of offence, but that it is part of an established discourse of power. As Mondal notes, "most of the time, offence is taken in relation to words, phrases, and tropes that have already been used to abuse and subordinate". And therefore the objection to abusive or offensive language is "not to the words themselves, nor even to the person uttering them in any given situation, but rather to the re-iteration of a power that has been deployed before".[71] These issues of power, subordination and offence will be explored in greater detail in the next chapter as we turn to Islamophobia and the role of free speech in legitimising civilisational discourse.

NOTES

1. Robin DiAngelo, "White Fragility", *International Journal of Critical Pedagogy* 3, no. 3 (2011): 59.
2. Kimberlé Williams Crenshaw, "Mark Lilla's Comfort Zone", *Baffler*, September 14, 2017, https://thebaffler.com/latest/mark-lillas-comfort-zone.
3. DiAngelo, "White Fragility", 60.
4. Joshua Paul, "'Not Black and White, but Black and Red': Anti-identity Identity Politics and #AllLivesMatter", *Ethnicities* 1, 19 (2019): 4.
5. DiAngelo, "White Fragility", 56.

6. Charles W. Mills, *The Racial Contract* (Ithaca, NY: Cornell University Press, 1997), 3.
7. Charles W. Mills, *Black Rights/White Wrongs: The Critique of Racial Liberalism* (Oxford: Oxford University Press, 2017), xv.
8. Robin D. G. Kelley, "Black Study, Black Struggle", *Boston Review*, March 7, 2016, http://bostonreview.net/forum/robin-d-g-kelley-black-study-black-struggle.
9. Crenshaw, "Mark Lilla's Comfort Zone".
10. Will Hutton, "Cecil Rhodes Was a Racist, but You Can't Readily Expunge Him from History", *Guardian*, December 20, 2015, https://www.theguardian.com/commentisfree/2015/dec/20/atonement-for-the-past-not-censorship-of-history.
11. PEN America, "And Campus for All: Diversity, Inclusion and Freedom of Speech at U.S. Universities", 6. https://pen.org/wpcontent/uploads/2017/06/PEN_campus_report_06.15.2017
12. Richard Delgaldo and Jean Stefancic, "Images of the Outsider in American Law and Culture: Can Free Expression Remedy Systemic Social Ills?" in *Critical Race Theory: The Cutting Edge*, ed. Richard Delgaldo and Jean Stefancic (Philadelphia: Temple University Press, 2013), 324.
13. Katie Rogers, "Pro-Trump Chalk Messages Cause Conflicts on College Campuses", *New York Times*, April 1, 2016, https://www.nytimes.com/2016/04/02/us/pro-trump-chalk-messages-cause-conflicts-on-college-campuses.html.
14. Bennett Carpenter, "Free Speech, Black Lives and White Fragility", *Duke Chronicle*, January 19, 2016, https://www.dukechronicle.com/article/2016/01/free-speech-black-lives-and-white-fragility.
15. Jelani Cobb, "Race and the Free Speech Diversion", *New Yorker*, November 10, 2015, https://www.newyorker.com/news/news-desk/race-and-the-free-speech-diversion.
16. Cohort of Middlebury Professors, "Letter from Middlebury Faculty", *Middlebury Campus*, March 2, 2017, https://middleburycampus.com/35336/opinion/letter-from-middlebury-faculty.
17. See Jeff McMahan, Francesca Minerva, and Peter Singer, "Setting the Record Straight on the '*Journal of Controversial Ideas*', *Guardian*, November 18, 2018, https://www.theguardian.com/world/2018/nov/18/setting-the-record-straight-on-the-journal-of-controversial-ideas.
18. "Discord at Middlebury: Students on the Anti-Murray Protests", *New York Times*, March 7, 2017, https://www.nytimes.com/2017/03/07/opinion/discord-at-middlebury-students-on-the-anti-murray-protests.html.
19. Cohort of Middlebury Professors, "Letter from Middlebury Faculty"; "Charles Murray at Middlebury: Unacceptable and Unethical, Say Over 500 Alumni", *Beyond the Green*, March 2, 2017, https://beyondthegreenmidd.wordpress.com/2017/03/02/charles-murray-at-middlebury-unacceptable-and-unethical-say-over-500-alumni/.
20. Allison Stanger, "Understanding the Angry Mob at Middlebury That Gave Me a Concussion", March 13, 2017, *New York Times*, https://www.nytimes.com/2017/03/13/opinion/understanding-the-angry-mob-that-gave-me-a-concussion.html
21. Cited in Taylor Gee, "How the Middlebury Riot Really Went Down", *Politico*, May 28, 2017, https://www.politico.com/magazine/story/2017/05/28/how-donald-trump-caused-the-middlebury-melee.
22. Bob Herbert writes, "I would argue that a group that was enslaved until little more than a century ago; that has long been subjected to the most brutal, often murderous, oppression; that has been deprived of competent, sympathetic political representation; that has most often had to live in the hideous physical conditions that are the hallmark of abject poverty; that has tried its best to survive with little or no prenatal care, and with inadequate health care and nutrition; that has been segregated and ghettoized in communities that were then redlined by banks and insurance companies and otherwise shunned by business and industry; that has been systematically frozen out of

the job market; that has in large measure been deliberately deprived of a reasonably decent education; that has been forced to cope with the humiliation of being treated always as inferior, even by imbeciles—I would argue that these are factors that just might contribute to a certain amount of social pathology and to a slippage in intelligence test scores"—Bob Herbert cited in Michael E. Staub, "The Mismeasure of Minds", *Boston Review*, May 8, 2019, http://bostonreview.net/race/michael-e-staub-mismeasure-minds.

23. David Gillborn, "Risk-Free Racism: Whiteness and So-Called 'Free Speech'", *Wake Forest Law Review*, 44 (2009): 536.

24. Keeanga-Yamahtta Taylor, *From #BlackLivesMatter to Black Liberation* (Chicago: Haymarket Books, 2016), 24–25.

25. Gillborn, "Risk-Free Racism", 554.

26. Staub, "The Mismeasure of Minds".

27. Angela Saini, "Why Race Science Is on the Rise Again", *Guardian*, May 18, 2019, https://www.theguardian.com/books/2019/may/18/race-science-on-the-rise-angela-saini.

28. "New Oxford Vice-Chancellor Urges 'Open-Minded' Students", BBC, January 12, 2016, https://www.bbc.co.uk/news/uk-england-oxfordshire-35290156.

29. Patrick Wolfe, *Traces of History: Elementary Structures of Race* (London: Verso, 2016), 40.

30. Delgaldo and Stefancic, "Images of the Outsider", 328.

31. Wolfe, *"Traces"*, 38.

32. Joshua Cohen, "Freedom of Expression", *Philosophy and Public Affairs* 22, no. 3 (1993): 232–33.

33. Brian Leiter, "The Case against Free Speech", 427n83.

34. Delgaldo and Stefancic, "Images of the Outsider", 328.

35. "The People vs 'the Elite'? State of Hate 2019", Hope Not Hate. https://www.hopenothate.org.uk/research/state-of-hate-report-2019/.

36. "Discord at Middlebury".

37. "Middlebury's Statement of Principle", *Wall Street Journal*, March 6, 2017, https://www.wsj.com/articles/middleburys-statement-of-principle-1488846993.

38. "Broken Inquiry on Campus: A Response by a Collection of Middlebury Students", *Broken Inquiry on Campus* (blog), March 12, 2017, https://brokeninquiryblog.wordpress.com.

39. Alan Howarth, *Free Speech* (London: Routledge, 1998), 1–2.

40. As Arun Kundnani writes in relation to dominant representations of terrorism, "The spectacle of the Muslim extremist renders invisible the violence of the US empire". The context is different but the logic is the same—Kundnani, *'The Muslims Are Coming!'* (London: Verso, 2015).

41. Joan Scott, "On Free Speech and Academic Freedom", *AAUP Journal of Academic Freedom* 8 (2017): 6.

42. Will Davies, "The Free Speech Panic: How the Right Concocted a Crisis", *Guardian*, July 26, 2018, https://www.theguardian.com/news/2018/jul/26/the-free-speech-panic-censorship-how-the-right-concocted-a-crisis.

43. See "Liberal Ghandi Fetishism", *Citations Needed* podcast, episode 74, https://citationsneeded.libsyn.com/episode-74-liberal-gandhi-fetishism-and-the-problem-with-pop-notions-of-violence.

44. Richard Cohen, "Protesters at Middlebury College Demonstrate 'Cultural Appropriation'—of Fascism", *Washington Post*, May 29, 2017, https://www.washingtonpost.com/opinions/protesters-at-middlebury-college-demonstrate-cultural-appropriation-of-fascism/2017/05/29.

45. Zack Beauchamp, "The New Reactionaries", *Vox*, February 26, 2019.

46. Alice Speri, "The Threat Within", *Intercept*, March 23, 2019, https://theintercept.com/2019/03/23/black-identity-extremist-fbi-domestic-terrorism.

47. Danielle Allen, "Why Middlebury's Violent Response to Charles Murray Reminded Me of the Little Rock Nine", *Washington Post*, March 7, 2017, https://www.washingtonpost.com/opinions/why-middleburys-violent-response-to-charles-murray-reminded-me-of-the-little-rock-nine/2017/03/07.

48. For a full account of the build-up to and reasons for the protest see Gee, "How the Middlebury Riot Really Went Down".

49. Mari J. Matsuda, "Public Response to Racist Speech: Considering the Victim's Story", in *Words That Wound: Critical Race Theory, Assaultive Speech, and the First Amendment*, ed. Charles R. Lawrence III, Mari J. Matsuda, Kimberlé Williams Crenshaw and Richard Delgado (London: Routledge, 1993), 77, ebook.

50. Laura Beth Nielsen, "Power in Public: Reactions, Responses, and Resistance to Offensive Public Speech", in *Speech and Harm: Controversies over Free Speech*, ed. Ishani Maitra and Mary Kate McGowan (Oxford: Oxford University Press, 2012), 153.

51. Ibid., 149.

52. Timothy Garton Ash, *Free Speech: Ten Principles for a Connected World* (London: Atlantic Book, 2016), 575–76, ebook.

53. Anshuman A. Mondal, *Islam and Controversy: The Politics of Free Speech after Rushdie* (London: Palgrave Macmillan, 2014), 26.

54. Ibid., 26.

55. See, for example, the reaction to Channel 4 News anchor Jon Snow reporting, at a pro-Brexit march, that he has never seen so many White people. Myriam François, "The Fury of 'White People' with Jon Snow Shows a Total Lack of Self-Awareness on Race". *Guardian*, April 12, 2019, https://www.theguardian.com/commentisfree/2019/apr/12/jon-snow-white-people-brexit-rally. See also, David Roberts, "American White People Really Hate Being Called 'White People'", *Vox*, July 26, 2018.

56. Jarett Kobek, *I Hate the Internet* (London: Serpent's Tale, 2016), 10.

57. DiAngelo, "White Fragility", 60–61.

58. Ibid., 59.

59. Mondal, *Islam and* Controversy, 6.

60. Mick Hume, *Trigger Warning: Is the Fear of Being Offensive Killing Free Speech?* (London: William Collins, 2015), 76, ebook.

61. Claire Fox, *'I Find That Offensive!'* (London: Biteback, 2016), 9, ebook.

62. Brendan O'Neill, "From No Platform to Safe Space: A Crisis of Enlightenment", in *Unsafe Space: The Crisis of Free Speech on Campus*, ed. Tom Slater (London: Palgrave, 2016), 16.

63. Ibid., 14.

64. Ishani Maitra and Mary Kate McGowan, "Introduction and Overview", in *Speech and Harm*, 16.

65. Frederick Schauer, "On the Distinction between Speech and Action", *Emory Law Journal* 65, no. 2 (2015): 428.

66. Lynne Tirrell, "Genocidal Language Games", in Maitra and McGowan, ed., *Speech and Harm*, 195, 175.

67. Catherine A. MacKinnon, "Foreword", in Maitra and McGowan, ed., *Speech and Harm*, xv.

68. Matsuda, "Public Response", 75, ebook.

69. Ibid., 76.

70. Matsuda cited in Ishani Maitra, "Subordinating Speech", in Maitra and McGowan, ed., *Speech and Harm*, 99.

71. Mondal, *Islam and Controversy*, 25.

Chapter Four

The War on Muslims

One of the key sites of both recent and historical free speech controversies and debates has been the supposed confrontation between the "Liberal West" and Islam. From the Salman Rushdie affair to the *Charlie Hebdo* massacre, free speech has frequently been invoked as the pivotal liberal democratic right to help preserve the West from the barbarians deemed to be waiting at, and climbing over, and blowing up, the gates. If we don't defend free speech, we hear, we'll all soon be subject to totalitarian Islamic rule, to sharia law and the end of civilisation as we know it. These people are not like us, they cry, and so must insult them, defame them, denigrate, vilify and silence them.

Muslims are probably the group of people most frequently and commonly targeted by free speech warriors. It is here that we can see the most egregious hypocrisy and double standards, and how blatantly self-serving and shamelessly contradictory many free speech defenders really are.[1] Free speech has been one of the most consistent go-to ruses for the justification of hate speech and other forms of discrimination against, and silencing of, Muslims. From Geert Wilders to Tommy Robinson, from new Atheists to certain liberal feminists, from the mainstream media to conspiracy theory websites, from the French to the United States government, free speech is repeatedly invoked in relation to Islam and Muslims, and in particular used as a means of promoting the very liberal values that are simultaneously denied to Muslims. Islam itself is seen as a threat to free speech, and woolly leftists defending Muslims against misrepresentation and Islamophobia are seen as a threat to free speech, and multiculturalism accommodating Islam is seen as a threat to free speech. Free speech, it is argued, is what distinguishes us from them. And free speech is what is needed to tell "difficult", uncomfortable truths about Muslims, or to have what anti-PC liberals describe as "important debates about immigration and Islam", which they claim have been "stifled" by the politically correct left.[2] We need courageous people to say out loud what apparently everyone else, or the silent majority, really thinks.

However, far from ever hearing anything truthful about Islam, almost everything written and said about Muslims in the Western media is at best profoundly biased and misleading, and at worse criminally inaccurate and incendiary, and either way serves a range of harmful ends. Furthermore, media representations of Islam and Muslims are usually framed in ways that predetermine and narrowly constrain almost all discussions—according to a reductive binary of good Muslim/bad Muslim or solely in relation to topics such as terrorism, immigration or radicalisation. These frameworks—which determine what news stories are selected, and how they are interpreted and situated within broader dominant narratives—are highly significant for establishing what is known about Muslims. Framing is one of the key "means by which minority populations have been simultaneously misrecognised and starved of adequate representations of themselves".[3] Citing data analysis, Des Freedman shows that media coverage of Muslims in Britain, for example, is framed in overwhelmingly negative terms, frequently focusing on terrorism or cultural differences, emphasising nouns such as *extremist*, *Islamist* and *suicide bomber* and adjectives such as *radical*, *fanatical* and *fundamentalist*. Islam and Muslims are regularly represented "in terms of a predisposition to violence" or as having "civilizational shortcomings". He concludes that Muslims therefore "appear to feature in the public imagination only in relation to their status as 'problems' and 'terrorists' and by virtue of having a different moral framework to non-Muslim British citizens".[4]

And yet this overwhelmingly negative public picture of Islam does little to stop people, including popular media commentators, from claiming that 'you can't criticize Islam' or that 'free speech is under threat over Islamophobia' and other such clichés.[5] Furthermore, little does it stop Islam from being criticised and 'debated' almost obsessively. And nor does it stop those that do criticise Islam, especially if done in an incendiary manner, from becoming media sensations or from receiving disproportionate media attention or even from building entire, often highly lucrative, careers.⁶ This can be witnessed repeatedly: a public figure says something outrageous and supposedly taboo-breaking about Islam, receives some mild pushback, then claims victim status and that free speech is being infringed by multicultural liberal metropolitan elites who are apologists for Islamo-facism and terrorism. They receive massive media coverage and become free speech heroes.

It is important to recognise that many such media controversies are the result not only of "media-savvy commentators whose broad access to a mainstream media hungry for cheap polemics has allowed them to publicise" their Islamophobic message,⁷ but well-established tactics and carefully planned strategising. They are part of what Nathan C. Lean refers to as the "Islamophobia industry", an industry whose "central figures and organisations [are] highly influential and increasingly central to the worldviews of leading political figures".⁸

This helps explain why so many of the views expressed about Islam are almost always the same, and not exclusive to the far right—they often derive from the same highly limited, but powerful pool of sources. The far right may express such views in more extreme terms and may advocate more extreme action, but the views are widely shared across the political spectrum. The English Defence League, for example, states that "Muslims can have their faith, that is their right, but when that faith infringes upon our hard fought freedoms, our democracy, our right to freedom of speech and expression then we will counter it at every opportunity because it is a threat to our way of life, our customs, our rule of law".⁹ This argument is warmed-over liberalism, the kind of thing uttered by politicians and the liberal commentariat on a regular basis. As Christine Delphy notes, the idea that Islam is incompatible with democracy has been a constantly reoccurring theme of the mainstream liberal media for decades.¹⁰

The argument performs a great deal of ideological work, as it presupposes and asserts a perceived binary between 'us' and 'them', and repeats the well-worn claim that Muslims constitute some kind of generalised threat, behind which lies an implicit or explicit set of accompanying claims: that Islam is inherently violent, that Muslims are responsible for terrorism or are all potential terrorists; that Islam is hideously patriarchal, paternalistic and mistreats women; that Islam is culturally backward and Muslims are inferior; that Muslims are homophobic; that Muslim men are sexual deviants or predators; that Islam is static and monolithic. As always it is important to consider who benefits from such narratives, what ideological and material investments people and institutions have in them, to examine where they come from and why they have so much staying power and why so many people so easily accept and disseminate them.

WHAT IS ISLAMOPHOBIA?

Islamophobia is not, and should not be viewed as, an organic, naturally occurring public reaction to perceived fears or threats from Islam. It is manufactured, orchestrated, whipped up and maintained (as, of course, is the idea that there is a free speech crisis). And it is done in multiple guises and from multiple political perspectives—from the left to the far right, since in many cases "the fight against Islam trump[s] any other political consideration".[11] There's nothing natural about racism; "it does not flow intrinsically and mysteriously from culture, colonialism or imperialism, nor equally vaguely from a capitalist or neoliberal 'racial order'". It always serves a purpose. Massoumi, Mills and Miller note that "ideas do not 'float freely', they are materially produced and disseminated by particular social actors with particular interests in the particular circumstances in which they find themselves". It is therefore crucial to recognise that "there are specific agents and institutions implicated in racist practices and in the production of Islamophobic ideas, policies and structures".[12] These include think tanks, academia, the media and right-wing social movements. The ideas they foster gain strength and the capacity to travel, notes Deepa Kumar, "to the degree that they coincide with material and political interests".[13] It is especially important, therefore, to recognise the role of the state in not only normalising and legitimising Islamophobia through its official discourse, but institutionalising and enshrining in law, policy and practice a raft of Islamophobic measures which, writes Arun Kundnani, enable both "the systematic violation of the rights of Muslims" and the "demonization of actions taken to remedy those violations".[14]

Kundnani argues that Islamophobia needs to be understood as the ideology of imperialism.[15] Islamophobia is central to the legitimisation of military interventions overseas, securitisation at home and, more broadly, the maintenance of liberalism and white supremacy as a ruling ideology. Muslims play the role of an 'ideal' or 'suitable' enemy, a group both perceived to be and represented as, most notoriously by Samuel Huntington, homogenous, racially and culturally distinct, and ideologically hostile.[16] As Kundnani writes, "A social body dependent on imperialist violence to sustain its way of life must discover an ideology that can disavow that dependency if it is to maintain legitimacy. Various kinds of racism have performed that role in the modern era; Islamophobia is currently the preferred form".[17] In the modern era, the construction of this ideological enemy can be traced back to at least the Iranian revolution. But it was 9/11 and the subsequent War on Terror which unleashed an obsessive preoccupation with the idea of Islam as a threat to the West. In both cases, a repository of myths from the European colonial legacies of Orientalism were drawn upon to foster, embellish and perpetuate this dominant narrative of a supposed clash of civilisations. But it is also important to recognise that Islamophobia fits into broader forms of racial discrimination. Islamophobia "is only possible", argues Kundnani, "because it resonates within the longer trajectories of racisms that are embedded in the social structures of the US" and Europe.[18]

As we saw in the previous chapter, a dominant form of racism is denial that it exists. In the case of anti-Muslim racism, many of the same people that make unfounded, essentialist, derogatory claims about Muslims deny that Islamophobia is racist or that it even exists,[19] claiming it is a propaganda term or left-wing conspiracy, used to silence sound rational criticisms, with some going so far as to claim that "those who denounce Islamophobia have armed the assassins".[20] It is argued that Islamophobia is not racism because Islam is a religion not a race. At best, this suggests, as Fred Halliday argued, that Islamophobia is an unhelpful term, as it conflates religion and race, and could be seen to prevent legitimate criticism of reactionary practices in Islam. For Halliday the prejudice is against Muslims as people (often the most secular, as in the case of Iraq) and not their faith.[21] Furthermore, it could be argued that by emphasising the element of irrational fear in racism, as evoked by 'phobia', it can make it seem as if Islamophobia is the result of individual psychology, some kind of mental disorder, which like arachnophobia is not really the fault of the individual, not something they can control, let alone the fault of the wider culture. It is the case that Islamophobes, like other racists, irrationally fear "others" (to see this, one needs only to consider the amount of times Muslim-'looking' or -'sounding' people have been asked to exit commercial airlines prior to take-off to allay white peoples' fears), but though understanding Islamophobia as a phenomenon of individual psychology, driven by fear and hatred of cultural difference, is important, a psychological focus is depoliticising and above all, prevents us from seeing the ways in which Islamophobia is a structural and systemic issue.[22]

The idea that the accusation of Islamophobia prevents criticism of Islam is baseless, since, firstly, Islamophobes criticise Islam all the time and, secondly, it is perfectly feasible to critique Islam as a religion without doing so in a racist manner. More importantly, however, the denial that Islamophobia is racist prevents an understanding of how it works. Islamophobia is not only racist because it targets ethnic minorities, which it does, but above all because Islam as a religion and Muslims as people are racialised. Understanding how this is done requires giving up the idea or assumption that religious affiliations are never to do with the body, and that 'race' is only to do with the body.[23] As Yassir Morsi notes,

> I know not of a culture divorced from its body. Islam in all its many manifestations does not separate itself neatly into a 'religious' idea that floats only in my head. It shaped my world before I was thrown into it. The Islamicate embodies my everyday practices: how I eat, talk, worship, look, dress and in what spaces I inhabit.[24]

Racialisation describes the process by which a group of people are made into a race on account of a set of supposed markers or characteristics which are perceived to define them as different. Steve Garner and Saher Selod write that "it entails ascribing sets of characteristics viewed as inherent to members of a group because of their physical or cultural traits", which are "not limited to skin tone or pigmentation, but include a myriad of attributes including cultural traits such as language, clothing, and religious practices".[25] This focus on essentialised cultural difference "in which Islam is made into a reified culture that bears an inherent 'nature' predisposing Muslims to certain behaviours" is central to the dominant mode of explaining Islamic terrorism and the supposed conflict between Islam and the West more generally. This mode in which "the problem is 'their' culture, not 'our' politics",[26] enables Western countries to disavow their own violence and the political reasons for acts of terrorism by displacing political antagonisms onto the plane of culture. In this way, argues Kundnani, all acts involving Muslims, whether terrorism related or not, are explained in terms of the racialised, fixed nature of the 'Other'.[27]

FREE SPEECH AS CIVILISATIONAL DISCOURSE

As we've seen in previous chapters, the racialisation of 'Others' is central to liberalism's self-conception, and Islamophobic discourses which figure the Muslim as part of a monolithic, unindividuated horde help to create and reinforce the liberal idea of the rational Western subject able to think and choose and speak freely. In this way we can see how "Islamophobia in its liberal guise appears as a defence of liberal values",[28] and that the invocation of free speech in relation to Islam operates as what Wendy Brown calls a "civilizational discourse", that is to say, a means of making a distinction between so-called civilised societies and those that are supposedly uncivilised or barbaric. Brown writes, "In the modern West, a liberal discourse of tolerance distinguishes 'free' societies from 'fundamentalist' ones, the 'civilized' from the 'barbaric', and the individualized from the organicist or collectivized".[29] This civilisational binary operates in such a way that whenever one pair of terms is present, it works metonymically to imply the others, so one need only invoke one word or value in the chain for a raft of positive and negative associations to come in its wake. Thus, when free speech is appealed to in relation to Islam, it implicitly asserts a binary between open, liberal, tolerant, rational, advanced, democratic societies and their opposite.

There are many of ways of attempting to dismantle this binary, which is little more than an infantile '*Star Wars*' view of the world, where there are only dark and light forces, and not, as is actually the case, a highly complex mix of races, ethnicities, cultures, religions, and nation-states overlapping and changing in a myriad of ways. One could dismantle it by appealing to a genealogical analysis, such as Edward Said's *Orientalism*, which would show that it is a historical and ideological construction, based on a specious and highly reductive notion of both the West and Islam; or to a historical analysis, such as Aimé Césaire's *Discourse on Colonialism*, which would show that by any measure Western countries have been the perpetrators of more barbarity, intolerance and backwardness than any country in the so-called Islamic world, that European colonialism, for example, worked "to decivilize the colonizer, to brutalize him in the true sense of the word, to degrade him, to awaken him to buried instincts, to covetousness, violence, race hatred, and moral relativism";[30] pulling him "deeper and deeper into the abyss of barbarism".[31] However doing so is unlikely to diminish its staying power, such is its centrality to liberalism's self-conception, for as Kundnani notes, "Islam is merely the absolute 'Other' that enables the construction of a positive image of oneself".[32]

At the centre of both liberalism and the liberal defence of free speech is the idea of the morally autonomous, rational, free individual. This individual stands in contrast to the kind of human subjects conceived of as belonging to nonliberal societies, who are thought to be determined by their culture. Brown writes, "'Culture' is what nonliberal peoples are imagined to be ruled and ordered by, liberal peoples are considered to have culture or cultures".[33] In other words, the liberal conceptions of both the West and of free speech rely not only on the idea that Western society is constituted by autonomous rational individuals, but that non-Western societies are culturally determined. This asymmetry, argues Brown, turns on an imagined opposition between culture and individual moral autonomy, in which the former vanquishes the latter unless culture is itself subordinated by liberalism through the use of rationality and will. Brown writes, "the liberal formulation of the individuated subject as constituted by rationality and will figures a non-individuated opposite who is so because of the underdevelopment of both rationality and will. For the organicist creature, considered to lack rationality and will, culture and religion (culture as religion, and religion as culture) are saturating and authoritative".[34] In other words, for liberalism to make sense it has to exclude culture from the realm of subject constitution and from politics. Culture in liberal societies is conceived as extrinsic to both individual identity and politics, whereas in nonliberal societies it is conceived as constitutive of both identity and politics. And yet Western culture is conceived by liberals as the highest achievement of humanity; that which has best allowed for human advancement. So Western culture is central to legitimising what 'we' do and who 'we' are, and yet it is merely something 'we' can choose to buy or opt into; it is not integral to who 'we' are. It is used as a means of justification at the same time that it is disavowed.

This opposition between rational individualism and religious conformism explains, in part, why new atheists such as Richard Dawkins or Sam Harris—leading figures in spreading and legitimising Islamophobia and leading advocates of the free speech defence—have such an obsession with religious others, especially Muslims.[35] The very existence of religious believers both threatens and confirms their conception of themselves as autonomous rational free agents. They need to repeatedly tell the story of how they have overcome what they figure as the childish constraints of culture and religion to become autonomous;

how they have moved on to a more advanced stage (though not so advanced that they can stop going on about how superior they are, or from indiscriminately bullying vulnerable minorities). Indeed, as Brown notes "the vanquishing of religion and culture is the very meaning of this autonomy".[36]

This account of the self and its relation to culture is particularly important to the autonomy-based defence of free speech, one of the central strands in liberal accounts of free speech. The problem with the account however is that, as Brian Leiter demonstrates, "the Kantian/Christian rhetoric about autonomy is a fiction: we are not autonomous beings". The idea that we are autonomous, which underpins not only liberal chauvinism, but also white male supremacy and the disavowal of its formation, privilege and structural advantage, presupposes a strict mind/body distinction, and requires abstracting and isolating deliberative rationality from embodied locations, constitutive practices and from historicized, cultured being.[37] But, as numerous philosophers and social scientists have shown, people in the West are no less cultured, embodied, situated and historicised than people elsewhere. As Griselda Pollock notes, "We all come embodied, located, classed, gendered, linguistically and ideologically captured by terms that cause us to be represented and represent ourselves in differences".[38] We are, states Leiter, "mostly artefacts of social, economic, and psychological forces beyond our control, mere vessels through which the various prejudices of our communities or personal histories pass", and as such, "we are not responsible for who we are" even though "who we are determines what we do, including what we say".[39] Furthermore, we are products of a socially constructed system in which some groups of people have been historically empowered and others systematically disempowered.

CHARLIE HEBDO AND THE RIGHT TO OFFEND

The use and invocation of free speech as a civilisational discourse was perhaps most in evidence in the reaction to the *Charlie Hebdo* massacre. The attack on *Charlie Hebdo* was widely perceived as an attack on free speech—an interpretation or framing that needs to be viewed as an iteration of George W. Bush's claim that 9/11 was an "attack on freedom itself" by "enemies of freedom" who "hate our freedoms: our freedom of religion, our freedom of speech, our freedom to vote and assemble and disagree with each other".[40] It may well be true that certain people in Middle Eastern countries and elsewhere hate the way the United States uses freedom as an empty ideological slogan in order to dissimulate and legitimise imperial acts of violence, occupation and wealth extraction, or hate their freedom to bomb other countries indiscriminately or to impose their neoliberal capitalist economic system on the world, leading to widespread deprivation and poverty. But it is difficult to imagine people hating an idea or principle. We should view this appeal to abstract ideological values as a means of deflecting attention away from the more concrete political reasons terrorism may occur.[41] The invocation of freedom or freedom of speech plays a crucial role in both depoliticising Muslim opposition to neo-colonial or imperial violence and contributing to the "dehumanising legitimation of violence against Muslims" in the Middle East and elsewhere.

Liberal, universalist discourses in a similar vein to Bush's response to 9/11 were once again drawn upon after *Charlie Hebdo*, as was the appeal to a civilisational binary between us and them. Politicians and media commentators in France and across the globe coalesced around the idea that it was an attack on freedom of speech, on France's republican universalism, and on French *laicite*. Given that it was an attack on journalists, such a framing of the event was understandable, but it became so dominant that it excluded any other possible interpretations and came to serve all sorts of ideological agendas: Firstly, "reducing the Charlie Hebdo attacks to a question of freedom of speech allow[ed] the government to ignore the disastrous socio-economic context in which some young French people become murderers";[42] secondly, it marginalised or suppressed any consideration of the wider political context of the global war on terror and ongoing violence in Iraq, Syria and elsewhere; and thirdly, it allowed the media to present themselves as "fearless defenders of free speech".[43] This fearlessness was most clearly trumpeted in the supposed right to offend.

One of the most common arguments made in defence of *Charlie Hebdo*'s decision to publish cartoons of the prophet Muhammad was the right to offend, an argument dear not only to many of the staunchest free speech absolutists (and the right to offend is merely free speech absolutism by another name), but the liberal centre more generally. After the massacre, displaying one's commitment to the right to offend was perceived as an act of solidarity. As Simon Dawes observes, "To say 'Je Suis Charlie', therefore, means not necessarily to approve of the content of the magazine, or to find it funny, or to condone racism, but to stand up for the right to offend, and for the right to blaspheme, in a secular and democratic republic".[44] Such commitment was often expressed in highly self-righteous terms, with numerous commentators arguing that causing offence is courageous and honourable, and publishing offensive cartoons the sign of true free expression. From across the media spectrum, it was argued that the right to offend is essential to freedom of speech, and therefore to civilisation, and human and social progress. If freedom is to mean anything, they proclaimed, it must include the freedom to offend.[45] In this way they echoed the free speech absolutist arguments of libertarians such as Brendan O'Neill, who claims that "offensiveness is a good thing. Blasphemy has benefits. The instinct to shock and upset society is often a positive one. In fact, it can be the motor of progress".[46] For O'Neill there is not only a right but a "duty" to offend, as if his obnoxious adolescent bullying is because of a deep-rooted Kantian concern for society and not because he is a professional troll.

The first thing to note about the right to offend is that, even though it is invoked all the time, there is actually no such thing; it is a fictitious right. It is not only that it comes into conflict with other rights and values such as the right to dignity and to live safe from harm, but it does not exist. One may have the right not to be prosecuted for offending someone (although it depends on the nature of the offence and the context), but that is not the same thing as the right to offend. In any case, proponents of the supposed right to offend justify it by claiming that, among other things, provocation leads to the sharpening of arguments and therefore to truth, and that offensiveness is a means of 'speaking truth to power'. No doubt this can be true, one need only think of satirists such as Jonathan Swift to see that, but most modern-day provocateurs, including *Charlie Hebdo*, have no wider vision of social justice in mind; they are provocative without being subversive. Their views and arguments are designed to do little more than generate outrage, or worse, to shore up liberal eurocentrism and white supremacist normativity; they give a supposedly radical veneer to reactionary ideas. In making their argument, the right-to-offend crowd posit all articulations of offensiveness as equivalent. They claim to be 'equal opportunity offenders', which is the basis of the idea or very tired cliché that the best antidote to offensive speech is more speech, and that "the 'marketplace of outrage' . . . is a neutral space devoid of power differentials".[47] This is the theory, at least, which itself is highly questionable, as it not only overlooks the glaring inequalities in society and the fact that only in some abstract fantasy world can offending the powerful be considered equivalent to bullying the disempowered, but it also, as we'll see below, reflects a failure to understand the way in which offence works, or what offence means. Furthermore, it demonstrates "a complete failure to understand the costs to members of the attacked group".[48] As Delphy notes of the media's defence of *Charlie Hebdo*'s Islamophobic brand of humour:

> None of the media bothered to mention that Islam is the religion or the culture of the most underprivileged and loathed people in France, regularly denounced by not-at-all subversive dailies and weeklies, and that it does not take much anti-conformism and even less courage to draw cartoons packed with racist jokes that Muslims—and Arab-looking people more generally—must suffer in silence every day of their lives.[49]

In practice, however, equal opportunity offenders and their defenders, insist that some forms of speech and behaviour are worse than others. This is all too evident in France, where insulting republican values or France itself or not properly respecting *Charlie* are all deemed to be much more offensive than Islamophobic slurs.[50] Immediately after the attacks, for example, people who resisted the call to openly embrace the official narrative of unequivocal support for *Charlie* were condemned and punished in various ways, such as the eight-year-old schoolchild taken to the police for refusing to say "*Je suis Charlie*". Indeed, the discrepancy between an avowed official commitment to universal equality and freedom and blatant forms of discrimination are highly evident in French law, and not solely as a reaction to *Charlie Hebdo*. The headscarf ban is perhaps the best-known example of this.[51]

The right to offend seems to be particularly important to people whose structural power makes it unlikely that they will experience effective offence themselves; those least likely to be offended by anything, not because they have thicker skin or are exceptionally open-minded, but because they belong to a privileged group whose structural advantage means they are unlikely to be impacted by anything that a person belonging to a less privileged group could say (apart, of course, from questioning the former's privilege). Likewise, in practice the right to offend is most often invoked to defend offending groups of people, such as Muslims, who have little or no right of reply, who because they lack equality in a larger social context have less freedom of speech, for, as Chris Demaske notes, free speech "necessarily rewards those for whom life is tolerably free already far more than those for whom emancipation remains in the future".[52] However, given their belief in the importance of free speech, right-to-offend advocates should be concerned that the speech of those with power (economic or otherwise) often silences the speech of those in less powerful positions, and that free speech is not equal or not equally distributed. The fact that it doesn't seem to concern them would suggest that free speech for these people is little more that "the right to bully, to mock and to stereotype without regard for the consequences".[53]

Defenders of offensive speech seem to want to have it both ways—that words do and don't have power. They claim that speech is not action, that words can't harm, as they are "ultimately just words", and so by implication that speech is not terribly important or consequential, and yet at the same time they insist that the pen is mightier than the sword, that speech is vital since it enables the pursuit of truth and allows progress and democracy to flourish and power to be held to account. Furthermore, according to their standard line of argument, stifling speech causes harm, yet speech itself doesn't. We need protection from the harm caused by silencing, but not from speaking. Their argument concerning the harmlessness of speech relies on the belief that words are devoid of any social, cultural or historical context and merely exist in isolation, which, as philosophers of language such as Wittgenstein and linguists such as Saussure have shown, is not the case. And as Glen Newey notes, "It's hard to see why speech can matter only in a good way: it can do so only if the one relevant aspect of speech is the act itself, rather than its effects". In other words speech would have to be conceived as *blurting*, in which talk matters mainly not to get something across, but to get it out, and therefore as having no consequences.[54] Such a conception of speech is in direct contradiction with free speechers' patron saint J. S. Mill, for whom the value of speech resides in its consequences.[55] Conceiving of speech as blurting, however, might explain why those that defend the right to offend are often the one's most indignant when people are indeed offended by offensive things they say—that is, by the consequences of their speech. They want to offend but become offended in turn if called out for it—blaming oversensitivity for the offence caused, rather than the offensive remarks. One would have thought that for offence to matter, it needs to be effective. If people are not offended by offensive remarks, then how offensive can the offensive remarks be? But if people *are* offended, then they are told to toughen up and not be such cry-babies (anti-PC offenders, like playground bullies, always like to double-down in their attacks).

The defence of offence has in part to be viewed as performative, as a demonstration of one's edgy credentials, of one's "intellectual daring"; it is invoked to suggest nonconformity, autonomous thinking, the refusal to bow down to institutional pressure; to challenge conventions; to situate oneself in a historical lineage of courageous speakers of truth to power, ranging from Galileo to Lenny Bruce. As John Durham Peters writes, free speech defenders "like to fancy themselves donning powdered wigs and taking quill in hand to compose declarations and encyclopaedias that will set tyrants trembling".[56] Invoking the power of offence permits free speech warriors to paint themselves in a heroic light as fearless challengers of established dogma, like the founding fathers of liberal free speech rights, which in part explains why they are still arguing as if threatened by a despotic monarchy censoring seditious pamphlets or, in the French case, "still living the anti-papist fight of a hundred years ago".[57] O'Neill writes, "A willingness to offend deeply entrenched ways of thinking, helped to deliver mankind from the Dark Ages into the relatively Enlightened societies many of us now inhabit",[58] a self-serving narrative that neatly maps onto the orientalist binary of the liberal West and Islam. Unlike the founding fathers or anti-clerical rebels, however, today's heroes have made careers from offending the vulnerable, oppressed and marginalised—transpeople, students, immigrants, and above all, Muslims. One would have thought that one sign of an enlightened society might be that there is no longer a need to shock and upset people, and that measuring freedom by the ability to offend rather than to enlighten is no sign of progress.[59] Indeed, it is difficult to see anything enlightened about most of today's provocateurs who seem to wallow in their own ignorance and take pleasure in offending for its own sake. Unsurprisingly, there is often a highly gendered aspect to this performance, for as Joan Scott notes,

> The bad boys can say anything they want, however vile and hateful: Yiannopoulos, Spencer, Charles Murray, Donald Trump. The worse the better, for it confirms their masculine prowess, their ability to subvert the presumed moralism of those they designate as "eggheads" and "snowflakes"—female-identified prudes who, in a certain stereotypical rendering of mothers, wives, and girlfriends, are the killjoys who seek to reign in the aggressive, unfettered sexuality that is the mark of their manly power.[60]

This conception of free speech as saying what you want and offending who you want is emblematic of a broader idea of liberal freedom, of the idea that individualised expression is the true area of freedom, the site of one's agency. This is how, paradoxically, such bad boys can promote themselves as defenders of democracy, for as Jennifer Peterson argues, "a fetishistic over-investment in speech and expressive 'freedom' helps create the feeling of a more perfect (egalitarian and pluralistic) democracy".[61] This feeling depends on the location of liberal freedom in the private or intimate realm, rather than the public realm of political economy or social justice. Casting expression as the primary realm of agency, claims Peterson, allows issues of economy and structure to be disavowed, and individuals to invest in only one level of social life as the realm of 'freedom'.[62] In this way, freedom of speech is a legitimising discourse that promotes a narrow and ideological conception of liberal freedom, of supposedly free and equal citizens operating in a marketplace of ideas. And within today's neoliberal marketplace "freedom is submitted to market meanings", and thus, argues Wendy Brown, it "is equated wholly with the pursuit of private ends, it is appropriately unregulated, and it is largely exercised to enhance the value, competitive positioning, or market share of a person or firm". And this is exactly why being offensive is so important to 'bad boys' such as Trump; it is a matter of enhancing brand value and gaining market share in the public sphere. It is in this way, argues Brown, that freedom and freedom of speech has "become the calling card and the energy of a manifestly unemancipatory formation".[63]

A common misconception of offence is that it concerns the use of certain 'bad' words, of exceeding the bounds of taste and decency, of failing to respect civility. Such a conception of offence is a key tool in the liberal policing of the public sphere; it is why calling Nigel Farage or Donald Trump or Boris Johnson a cunt is perceived to be more offensive or at least less permissible in public broadcasts than their divisive racist dog whistling and worse. But offence does not lie in certain words; no word is inherently offensive. That is not how language works, since words can be repurposed. Swear words, for example, can be and often are used as terms of affection. What matters is the context, and above all the question of power. As Mondal shows, "offensiveness is not produced by speaking certain inherently offensive words, but in the relationship between the speaker, the manner of the speech, the recipient, and the power relations that govern this relationship within the context of a given situation".[64] He writes, "What is being performed in the giving or taking of offence is power or, rather, to be more precise, the positioning of oneself in a power relation".[65]

But crucially, it is not necessarily a display of the speaker's individual power, but the power of the discourse used by the speaker. A person does not need to be powerful or in a position of power to be offensive, for it is by using a given discourse, such as racist speech, that power is asserted. Ishani Maitra illustrates this in relation to everyday racist speech to explain how speech can not only cause but constitute subordination; she shows that authority to subordinate need not derive from a speaker's social position, but can be assumed through the act of speaking racial slurs.[66] This is why a black person saying the n-word is different to a white person doing so, which is not to say that the meaning or use or offensiveness of this word is straightforward. The word can be used in multiple ways and registers, but what determines its offensiveness is the context. The word is offensive not only because of its history and the history of anti-Black racism and the use of derogatory language to legitimise and perpetuate a system of discrimination and violence, but because its use can be an attempt to assert one's superiority over another. Mondal writes, "Wounding words possess the power to hurt precisely because they have a history of violence behind them, both verbal and physical . . . that are part of an established discourse of power". And thus, "the perniciousness of racism lies in the continuing availability and purchase of racial discourse as a means of positioning oneself within established hierarchies of domination over racial others, and the reinforcement of such hierarchies in each successive iterative performance".[67]

This is why dominant groups not only can ignore offensive speech actions more easily than subordinate groups, they can also give offence much more easily too, and hence why claims of so-called reverse racism or equal opportunity offence are not only false but ideological. And this is why arguments about the right of the Western media to insult and offend Islam are so often misguided, disingenuous and false. The rationalisation of the value and necessity of offensiveness as a means of contesting power, which relies on an evacuation of power relations, is itself, argues Mondal, "a gesture that masks the dominance of western liberalism within the global economy of power".[68]

MUSLIM VOICES

In the Western media, Muslim voices are rarely heard, and Islam and Muslims are rarely given fair representation; indeed, there is a clear pattern of exclusion and misrepresentation. Muslims are overwhelmingly represented in a negative light, and not merely in news media, but also in cultural texts such as Hollywood films, TV series and novels. These representations matter. For vast swathes of the non-Muslim population, it constitutes how and what they know about Islam and Muslims. It determines how Muslims are seen and therefore how they are treated, or more likely, mistreated. The dominant forms of knowledge about Islam and Muslims are completely warped. Most people know nothing or worse than nothing—a heap of prejudicial and bogus talking points.

One of the ironies here is that a true defender of free speech should be deeply concerned about misrepresentation and the failure of any members of society to be heard. One of Mill's central claims in his defence of free speech concerns the tyranny of the majority or the tyranny of public opinion—a "tyranny more formidable than many kinds of political oppression, since . . . it leaves fewer means of escape, penetrating much more deeply into the details of life, and enslaving the soul itself".[69] Furthermore, if certain views or perspectives are not given fair representation, are not heard, this damages not only the holder of those views, but society more generally as it is deprived of the diversity of opinion which, argues Mill, is necessary to pursue the good life. It is also highly damaging to the process of democracy, which requires an informed citizenry.

One of the main defences of free speech is that speech restrictions lead to a "chilling effect", causing individuals to be "more fearful, and thus more careful and conformist in what they dare to say", likely to result in more restrained and homogenous expression.[70] Muslims, as well as other marginalised or oppressed groups, are restrained in how they speak and act publicly, but this is not something that seems to concern free speech warriors, who in many cases contribute to the climate of fear that Muslims are forced to inhabit. Thus, there is a twofold discrimination at work: not only is the freedom of speech of Muslims not taken into consideration but it is actively hindered. It might be the case that if you are unable to communicate in normal channels, if your arguments are not heard, if you are not only silenced, but repeatedly denigrated, dehumanised and insulted, and if you understand that the consequences of this misrepresentation are all too real and material, that they result in the indiscriminate oppression or even mass murder of innocent people, then you might feel compelled to resort to desperate measures. Anti-PC liberals, for example, argue that racists need to be heard because it will supposedly make the world a safer place, referring to data analysis showing that "countermeasures intended to constrain radical right politics appear to fuel extreme right violence", and therefore that allowing grievances to be voiced might prevent a turn to violence.[71] Such reasoning seems to overlook the fact that there is a problem with racism in the first place, suggesting that only extreme violence is the problem. It also overlooks the broader, more pervasive set of dangers radical right politics leads to, such as creating a more threatening hostile environment for minority groups. Furthermore, the same people are curiously silent on the countermeasures intended to constrain non-white radical groups; they do not argue that Islamic terrorism is caused by the suppression of Muslim's free speech or the restrictions imposed on their freedom, or that radical Muslims should be given platforms to voice their grievances. Indeed, many of the anti-PC liberals calling for far-right voices to be heard are quite happy for Muslim's free speech to be restricted and repeatedly espouse Islamophobic views.

The chilling effect on the Muslim community is not solely or even mostly a result of speech restrictions (though these certainly exist), but by more pervasive forms of social, cultural and political pressure and policing. Initially, there is the pressure of being perceived to represent all Muslims, to have to speak on behalf of Islam, to have to condemn every terrorist act in the terms deemed appropriate by the Western media. Any form of equivocation or attempt at explanation is considered beyond the pale. This feeds into a broader pressure to be what Mahmood Mamdani calls a "good Muslim". Post 9/11 "unless proved to be 'good', every Muslim was presumed to be 'bad'. All Muslims were now under obligation to prove their credentials by joining in a war against 'bad' Muslims".[72] If one is not perceived to be a good Muslim, that necessarily makes you a bad Muslim, which is to say, terrorist or terrorist sympathiser, a fundamentalist. In *Radical Skin/Moderate Masks* Yassir Morsi writes of this compulsion to become a good Muslim and all that has to be denied or erased from one's sense of self, and the "humiliating practice of chasing" one's identity, when the white gaze is one's reference. He reflects on the "dehumanising ways by which the War on Terror portrays the Muslim" and how Muslims have to "police the cultural excesses found in [them]selves".[73] In the context of the war on terror, there is no neutral standpoint for politically engaged Muslims. The hegemonic framework, or the white gaze, is always positioning the Muslim in some way, and usually in highly reductive ways. The effect of this is not only damaging to individual Muslims but is profoundly depoliticising.

More importantly, though, it is not just their speech or their right to speech that has been threatened, it has been their freedom in general. And not freedom in the empty, specious sense it is so often used to refer to liberal lives, but in the very real sense that their existence is subject to all sorts of curtailments, threats and violations. Since 9/11 and throughout the world, Muslims or even people perceived to be Muslims (which is to say those that match the stereotypical racial profile) have been subject to a raft of injustices and mistreatments—from profiling to hate crimes, false imprisonment to extradition, indiscriminate murder to torture. While liberals are hand-wringing over a manufactured free speech crisis, Muslims are the subject of increasingly illiberal treatment, which comes in the forms of institutional, structural and everyday racism and abuse.

Muslims are portrayed as a threat to civilisation and to liberal values, and yet it is precisely the treatment of Muslims that most clearly undermines such values. As Liz Fekete shows in *A Suitable Enemy*, the threat to our 'values' "comes from a domestic peril of Europe's own making". And it derives from the way that the supposed danger and threat of both terrorism and immigration is conceived and, hence, countered: "it is inherent in the counter-terrorism measures the EU has adopted since September 11, which extend the definition of terrorism, and in the emergency laws passed by member states so as to undermine the fundamentals of justice". And it is "based on a concept of national security that is shot through with xeno-racism".[74] This leads to a curious contradiction in which liberal states "engage in extra-legal and persecutorial actions toward the very group that it calls upon the citizenry to be tolerant toward".[75]

The liberal values of freedom, equality and justice are being championed at the very same time as these values are being denied to vast swathes of the population. In Europe and the United States increasingly draconian policies and laws have been adopted, or existing laws have been "misused", such as racial profiling and mass preventive detention, against their Muslim populations.[76] It is almost as if the more liberal democracies protest their liberal credentials, the more they feel entitled to betray them, or rather the more they betray them, the more they need to be seen to promoting them. Such hypocrisy of course has a long history; it is the logic and ideology of colonialism, what Morsi describes as European's "fantasy of civility" meant to "solve their original barbarity".[77] It is preaching "enlightenment humanism at the colonized" while denying it in practice.[78] Not only are liberal rights being denied to Muslim subjects but, Nisha Kapoor shows, Muslims are being subject to "colonial disciplinary techniques" that, though reconfigured, have been increasingly institutionalised by supposedly liberal democratic states such as Britain, France and the United States.[79]

The fact that they largely get away with this hypocrisy testifies not only to their power, but also to the power of dominant narratives. The way a State represents both its history and its values can shape the way people see it. France, Britain and the United States all excel in this regard, relying on a range of stock narratives, selective historical episodes, heroic figures, endlessly regurgitated slogans and ideological mythologising to present themselves as leading nations of freedom, equality and progress, while disavowing their historic and continuing role in violent and often criminal behaviour: from torture to exploitation, invasion to subjugation. All three disavow that their liberal identities "emerged through historic practices of empire building" and that the democratic ideals they so frequently trumpet "gained strength and meaning through frameworks of exclusion".[80] All three nations are built on false narratives. But the belief in these narratives—that, for example they are the lands of freedom or opportunity or fair play or equality and fraternity or human rights—is so deep rooted that whenever inconvenient facts get in the way they are easily dismissed. All one need do is repeat the mantra that one is good. For the *locus classicus* of this approach think of Tony Blair's shameless declaration that "I think most people who have dealt with me think I am a pretty straight sort of guy, and I am". Yes Tony, if you say so.

It could be argued, of course, that the disgraceful treatment and systemic silencing of Muslims in Western countries illustrates precisely why better free speech protection is required. The US Patriot Act, UK Prevent duty and the French outlawing of the veil all testify to egregious government overreach. It is clear that more needs to be done to protect the free speech of Muslim populations; more importantly, much needs to be done to amplify their voices, to shatter reductive stereotypes, tokenistic representation and narrowly circumscribed opportunities for public discourse. But a general defence of free speech as a principle and free speech absolutism will do nothing to alter the current distribution of power and forms of mainstream representation, nothing to alter the normalisation of Islamophobia, the institutionalisation of colonial disciplinary techniques, the policing and scapegoating of, and discrimination and violence against, Muslim populations. The free speech story and the role it plays in liberal democratic nations' self-congratulatory narratives needs to be challenged, not uncritically celebrated, as it helps mask these outrageous practices and prevents a more clear-sighted view of the actual issues. As poet Suhaiymah Manzoor-Khan writes,

> Britain is barbaric—
> . . .
> Britain is blood on its hands and back-to-the-wall
> Britain is selling weapons to the most repressive regimes in the world
> Britain is the bombs the Saudis drop on Yemen
> Britain is building surveillance apparatus since 9/11
> Britain is believing in human rights whilst removing them all.
> . . .
> Britain is suicide attempts, secret courts and secret torture
> Britain is stopping you at the border
> Britain is blaming the kids who aren't white
> Britain is blaming the immigrants
> Britain is blaming the Muslims
> . . .
> Britain is not that great.[81]

NOTES

1. See Mehdi Hasan, "As a Muslim, I'm Fed Up with the Hypocrisy of the Free Speech Fundamentalists", *New Statesman*, December 1, 2015, https://www.newstatesman.com/mehdi-hasan/2015/01/muslim-i-m-fed-hypocrisy-free-speech-fundamentalists; see alsohttps://paper-bird.net/2015/02/19/hypocrisy-and-free-speech.

2. Roger Eatwell and Matthew Goodwin, *National Populism: The Revolt against Liberal Democracy* (London: Pelican, 2018), 74.

3. Cited in Des Freedman, "Media Power and the Framing of the *Charlie Hebdo* Attacks", in *After Charlie Hebdo: Terror, Racism and Free Speech*, ed. Gavan Titley, Des Freedman, Gholam Khiabany and Aurélien Mondon (London: Zed Books, 2017), 211.

4. Freedman, "Media Power", 214.

5. Peter Hitchens, "Free Speech Is under Threat over Islamophobia", *Times*, March 26, 2019, https://www.thetimes.co.uk/article/free-speech-is-under-threat-over-islamophobia.

6. Nathan C. Lean documents that professional Islamophobes—people who run anti-Islamic websites or campaigns—such as Pam Geller and Robert Spencer earn annual salaries of over $200,000. The former for ten hours work a week. "Mainstreaming Anti-Muslim Prejudice: The Rise of the Islamophobia Industry in American Electoral Politics", in *What Is Islamophobia? Racism, Social Movements and the State*, ed. Narzanin Massoumi, Tom Mills and David Miller (London: Pluto Press, 2017), 127–28.

7. Aurélien Mondon and Aaron Winter, "*Charlie Hebdo*, Republican Secularism and Islamophobia", in Titley et al., *After Charlie Hebdo*, 37.

8. Lean, "Mainstreaming Anti-Muslim Prejudice", 124.
9. From EDL website, cited in Yassir Morsi, *Radical Skin, Moderate Masks: De-radicalising the Muslim and Racism in Post-racial Societies* (London: Rowman & Littlefield, 2017), 104.
10. Christine Delphy, *Separate and Dominate: Feminism and Racism after the War on Terror* (London: Verso, 2015), 13.
11. Mondon and Winter, *"Charlie Hebdo"*, 39.
12. Narzanin Massoumi, Tom Mills and David Miller, "Introduction: What Is Islamophobia?" in Massoumi, Mills and Miller, *What Is Islamophobia?*, 6.
13. Deepa Kumar, "Islamophobia and Empire: An Intermestic Approach to the Study of Anti-Muslim Racism", in Massoumi, Mills and Miller, *What Is Islamophobia?*, 67.
14. Arun Kundnani, *'The Muslims Are Coming!'* (London: Verso, 2015), 32.
15. Kumar, "Islamophobia and Empire", 50.
16. Kundnani, *Muslims*, 10; see also Liz Fekete, *A Suitable Enemy* (London: Pluto Press, 2009).
17. Kundnani, *Muslims*, 11.
18. Kundnani, "Islamophobia as Ideology of US Empire", in Massoumi, Mills and Miller, *What Is Islamophobia?*, 40.
19. For a recent example, see the controversy surrounding Roger Scruton, who claims *Islamophobia* is a propaganda word invented by the Muslim Brotherhood. Martin Kent, "Roger Scruton Claims He Is the Victim of a 'Right Wing Witch Hunt' as Row over New Statesman Interview Continues", *INews*, April 26, 2019, https://inews.co.uk/news/roger-scruton-george-eaton-new-statesman-spectator-interview-bbc-today-programme.https://inews.co.uk/news/roger-scruton-george-eaton-new-statesman-spectator-interview-bbc-today-programme.
20. Jeannette Bougrab cited in Nicholas De Genova, "The Whiteness of Innocence: Charlie Hebdo and the Metaphysics of Anti-Terrorism in Europe", in Titley et al., *After Charlie Hebdo*, 101.
21. Fred Halliday, "'Islamophobia' Reconsidered", *Ethnic and Racial Studies* 22, no. 5 (1999): 898–900.
22. Kundnani, "Islamophobia as Ideology", 36–37.
23. Steve Garner and Saher Selod, "The Racialization of Muslims: Empirical Studies of Islamophobia", *Critical Sociology* 41, no. 1 (2015): 11.
24. Yassir Morsi, *Radical Skin, Moderate Masks: De-radicalising the Muslim and Racism in Post-racial Societies* (London: Rowman & Littlefield, 2017), 11.
25. Garner and Selod, "Racialization", 12.
26. Kundnani, "Islamophobia as Ideology", 35.
27. Arun Kundnani, "Islamophobia: Lay-ideology of US-Led Empire", accessed May 11, 2019.
28. Mondon and Winter, *"Charlie Hebdo"*, 31.
29. Wendy Brown, *Regulating Aversion: Tolerance in the Age of Identity and Empire* (Princeton, NJ: Princeton University Press, 2006), 177.
30. Aimé Césaire, *Discourse on Colonialism* (New York: Monthly Review Press, 2000), 35.
31. Robin D. G. Kelley, "Introduction: A Poetics of Anti-Colonialism", in Césaire, *Discourse on Colonialism*, 8–9.
32. Kundnani, "Islamophobia".
33. Brown, *Regulating*, 150.
34. Ibid., 153.
35. See Narzanin Massoumi, Tom Mills and David Miller, "Liberal and Left Movements and the Rise of Islamophobia", in Massoumi, Mills and Miller, *What Is Islamophobia?*, 240–47.
36. Brown, *Regulating*, 153.

37. Ibid., 152.
38. Griselda Pollock, *Vision and Difference* (London: Routledge, 1988), xxvi.
39. Brian Leiter, "The Case against Free Speech", *Sydney Law Review* 38 (2016): 423–25.
40. George W. Bush, "President Bush Addresses the Nation", *Washington Post*, September 20, 2001, https://www.washingtonpost.com/wp-srv/nation/specials/attacked/transcripts/bushaddress_092001.html.
41. For example, Robert Pape shows "that there is little connection between suicide terrorism and Islamic fundamentalism, or any one of the world's religions. . . . Rather, what nearly all suicide terrorist attacks have in common is a specific secular and strategic goal: to compel modern democracies to withdraw military forces from territory that the terrorists consider to be their homeland"—Robert Pape, *Dying to Win: The Strategic Logic of Suicide Terrorism* (New York: Random House 2006), 4.
42. Philippe Marlière, "The Meaning of 'Charlie': The Debate on the Troubled French Identity", in Titley et al., *After Charlie Hebdo*, 53.
43. Freedman, "Media Power", 219.
44. Simon Dawes, "Charlie Hebdo and the Right to Offend", *openDemocracy*, January 21, 2015, https://www.opendemocracy.net/en/can-europe-make-it/charlie-hebdo-and-right-to-offend.
45. Jodie Ginsberg, "The Right to Free Speech Means Nothing without the Right to Offend", *Guardian*, February 16, 2015, https://www.theguardian.com/commentisfree/2015/feb/16/free-speech-means-nothing-without-right-to-offend-paris-copenhagen.
46. Brendan O'Neill, "Restore the Right to Offend", https://brendanoneill.co.uk/post/107600481429/restore-the-right-to-offend.
47. Anshuman A. Mondal, *Islam and Controversy: The Politics of Free Speech after Rushdie* (London: Palgrave Macmillan, 2014), 26.
48. Simon Lee, *The Cost of Free Speech* (London: Faber, 1990), 42.
49. Delphy, *Separate*, 21.
50. See, for example the case of Saïd Bouamama and Saïdou, who were indicted for 'public insult' for their anti-colonialist and anti-racist song and manifesto "Fuck France" ("Nique la France"). For an analysis of this hypocrisy in the context of normalised Islamophobia in France, see De Genova, "The Whiteness of Innocence", 102–6.
51. The logic of the headscarf ban takes some beating. We, the nation-state, want you, already assumed to somehow not belong, to be free. This involves you being like us. So to be free we must stop you from behaving as you want. Because what you think you want is not what you really want. We know what you really want. You want to be like us. Because we are free. You, unlike us, have been indoctrinated. You have no agency. We have agency. We are all individuals, you are not. You are a group. To be an individual you have to be and look like us, or at least not look like you.
52. Chris Demaske, *Modern Power and Free Speech: Contemporary Culture and Issues of Equality* (Lanham, MD: Lexington Books, 2009), 12.
53. Freedman, "Media Power", 219.
54. Glen Newey, "Unlike a Scotch Egg", *London Review of Books*, December 5, 2013, https://www.lrb.co.uk/v35/n23/glen-newey/unlike-a-scotch-egg.
55. Leiter, "Case against Free Speech", 430.
56. John Durham Peters, *Courting the Abyss: Free Speech and the Liberal Tradition* (Chicago: University of Chicago Press, 2005), 1.
57. Delphy, *Separate*, 19.
58. O'Neill, "Restore the Right to Offend".
59. Freedman, "Media Power", 219.
60. Joan Scott, "On Free Speech and Academic Freedom", *AAUP Journal of Academic Freedom* 8 (2017): 5.

61. Jennifer Peterson, "Freedom of Expression as Liberal Fantasy: The Debate over *The People vs. Larry Flynt*", *Media, Culture & Society* 29, no. 1 (2007): 378.

62. Ibid., 376.

63. Wendy Brown, "Neoliberalism's Frankenstein: Authoritarian Freedom in Twenty-First Century 'Democracies'", *Critical Times* 1, no. 1 (2019): 62.

64. Mondal, *Islam and* Controversy, 23.

65. Ibid.

66. Ishani Maitra, "Subordinating Speech", in *Speech and Harm: Controversies over Free Speech* ed. Ishani Maitra and Mary Kate McGowan (Oxford: Oxford University Press, 2012), 94–118.

67. Ibid., 25–26.

68. Mondal, *Islam and Controversy*, 26.

69. J. S. Mill, *On Liberty*, ed. Stefan Collini (Cambridge: Cambridge University Press, 1989), 8.

70. Judith Wagner DeCew, "Free Speech and Offensive Expression", in *Freedom of Speech*, ed. Ellen Frankel Paul, Fred D. Miller Jr. and Jeffrey Paul (Cambridge: Cambridge University Press 2004), 83.

71. Jacob Aasland Ravndal, "Explaining Right-Wing Terrorism and Violence in Western Europe: Grievances, Opportunities and Polarization", *European Journal of Political Research* 57 (2018): 847.

72. Mahmood Mamdani, *Good Muslim, Bad Muslim: America, The Cold War, and the Roots of Terror* (New York: Three Leaves Press, 2005), 27.

73. Morsi, *Radical Skin*, 11–12.

74. Fekete, *Suitable Enemy*, 43.

75. Brown, *Regulating*, 84.

76. Katherine Gelber, *Free Speech after 9/11* (Oxford: Oxford University Press, 2016), 101.

77. Morsi, *Radical Skin*, 5.

78. Dipesh Chakrabarty, *Provincializing Europe: Postcolonial Thought and Historical Difference* (Princeton, NJ: Princeton University Press, 2000), 4.

79. Nisha Kapoor, *Deport, Deprive, Extradite: 21st Century State Extremism* (London: Verso, 2018), 165.

80. Aziz Rana, *The Two Faces of American Freedom* (Cambridge, MA: Harvard University Press, 2010), 7–8.

81. Suhaiymah Manzoor-Khan, "British Values", in *Postcolonial Banter* (Birmingham, UK: Verve Poetry Press, 2019). Spoken version here: https://www.youtube.com/watch?v=lkDoTGCD2-g.

Chapter Five

Silencing

To be against free speech is not merely to be against the misuse of free speech as an ideological tool, it is also to be in favour of some forms of silencing. More precisely, it is to recognise that silencing and censorship occur all the time in liberal democratic societies, and that in some cases this is perfectly justified while in other cases it is not, but that free speech arguments are largely irrelevant in either case. The free speech brigade like to argue that silencing or censorship or any other forms of infringement on unrestrained free speech is bad in itself. Indeed, they like to throw words such as *censorship* around in ways that are often little more than propaganda, but highly effective propaganda. It is a cherished and largely unquestioned dogma that speech is good and silencing is bad. And so, for example, we repeatedly hear that "defending the rights of racists to speak is not the same thing as defending those ideas" and that "one's commitment to free speech matters most when it involves ideas you strongly oppose". What is being defended here is the abstract principle, regardless of consequences. This is what Catherine MacKinnon calls the "inverse arithmetic of free speech (the less you favour its content, the more you must support its existence)", which she argues, is one of the orthodoxies that "give 'speech' hegemony over all other rights and values".[1]

It is also important to defend offensive speech, we hear, because it could be the speech you make that is targeted next. It is essential "to stand up for the speech rights of fascists, racists, Islamists and pornographers", writes Brendan O'Neill, "not because those groups' ideas are valuable, but because when institutions assume the power to destroy moral viewpoints that are 'problematic', then it's only a matter of time before the freedom of respectable people is curbed, too".[2] This is classic slippery slope stuff, in which "it's only a matter of time" suffices as an argument, even though exactly why "respectable people's" freedom might end up being curbed is not clear. The problem with slippery slope arguments, as Simon Lee notes, is that not only are we already on the slope, as there are dozens of laws restricting free speech (copyright, intellectual property, misleading advertisements, libel, slander, official secrets, the list goes on), but there is no automatic slide to censorship as a result of them or any new ones coming into effect.[3] Slippery slope arguments presume a reductive binary between "complete freedom of speech or complete censorship", even though these are never the only options.[4] As John Durham Peters notes, "there is more space for life and thought than the simple choice between censorship and openness would suggest".[5]

Censorship, like many other morally loaded terms frequently used in place of argument, is invoked as a terrifying bogeyman used as an ever-present threat about what could happen if; its invocation operates to shut down discussion not enable it. The villain is typically some imaginary censorship bureau, a totalitarian government that can outlaw speech overnight, arbitrarily determining what constitutes offensive speech, and offence is viewed as a subjective form of expression unrelated to context or structure or power or history. One of the problems with this line of thinking is that, although it is commonly perceived as inherently bad, in practical terms censorship is utterly ordinary, used all the time in multiple ways, and most people support it.

Most people in liberal democracies are already against free speech, if by free speech is meant the unfettered absolute right to say what we want when we want to whom we want, in which all context, custom, taboo and civic sense is ignored. Which is to say, in practical terms and in concrete settings (and there aren't any others), most "reasonable, rational" people are in favour of, or implicitly consent to, controlled and policed speech, as well as to many forms of censorship. It is not merely that people are against such things as child pornography and incitement to violence, but that they consent in all sorts of ordinary ways to the way in which language use, like social behaviour more generally, is rule and norm governed, and so policed. In liberal democratic societies speech is controlled and restricted in all sorts of ways: by law, by social norms as well as by the fact that the right to free speech is necessarily in conflict with other rights and values. In other words, forms of silencing, censorship and language policing happen all the time and are perfectly ordinary. Indeed, not only are they ordinary but they are necessary for the functioning of civic society, for all the specific and different circumstances, situations, settings and institutions in which we operate with language. Almost all speech situations are governed by rules, codes, habits and customs, and they feature boundaries of acceptable and unacceptable speech as well as appropriate or relevant or intelligible speech. This is not to suggest that we are not free to act as we might want in a given speech situation; it is to argue that such freedom is largely irrelevant. In practical terms it has little bearing on how one acts and what one says in any given situation. In a law court or university seminar room or church or football stadium or gym we speak in different ways and for different purposes. If we want to participate in meaningful discussion or meaningful interaction in any given setting, we implicitly consent to the norms and rules, to the restrictions governing it. Speech would be meaningless if this did not occur. Therefore, what matters is not that we have a right to free speech, but how we use it.

Arguing in favour of silencing, however, is a challenge, as many people are deeply suspicious of even the idea of it, for "no one wants to look like a fan of censorship".[6] And, to some extent, with good reason. The history of silencing and censorship is full of egregious abuses of power, paranoid control freaks and barbaric acts of policing, but so is the history of capitalism and you don't hear many free speech absolutists calling for its abolition. Being against censorship is a surefire way to claim the moral high ground, notes Peters, who reminds us of the way free speech defenders "lather themselves into a righteous fury against censorship; and bystanders eager to not be associated with the powers of darkness find themselves cheering on the spectacle of fearless souls speaking truth to power".[7] But such theatre is all the more reason not to overlook the importance of censorship and silencing. The fact is that restrictions can be and often are good, even necessary. As Brian Leiter states, "Western liberal democracies are rife with institutions that view massive restrictions on speech as essential to realising the ends of free societies"—not least law courts. "There is no free speech in the courtroom and (almost) no one thinks there should be".[8] Similarly, P. G. Ingram argues that "according to the case in question, restrictions on free speech may be seen as beneficial rather than detrimental, as necessary and desirable for society and not just expedient for the state or government".[9] In many areas of our shared life restrictions not only makes our lives easier, better and more practical but can even save lives.

POWER

Restrictions, silencing and censorship are not the main threat to free speech in liberal democratic societies. Of much greater significance is how much purchasing power one has in the 'marketplace of ideas'; what matters is which voices are heard and are dominant in the public realm; what speech is amplified and normalised, and what voices and ideas are excluded. De facto censorship, silencing and policing happens in all sorts of ways, largely dictated not by governments but a combination of economic forces and civic values and social norms. Standards of what is socially acceptable are just as powerful as economic factors in determining what and how we communicate. As Lee argues, "Threats to free speech come from all directions", and mostly from the privatized, corporate sphere, not the public one.[10] So, for example, radical leftist speech may not be censored but can be policed in a raft of other, often much more effective, ways. Certain ideas are routinely dismissed as unrealistic or certain words become unsayable, or are associated with terrorism or totalitarianism. Even scientific ideas, such as the incontrovertible truth of climate change, can be denied by the power and influence of corporate and media interest. For example, though scientific experts and international panels agree on the human causes of climate change, nonetheless, in the United States less than 50 percent of people believe it.[11] More importantly, social norms are often racist and sexist, they privilege whiteness and maleness, and do so in a range of subtle and not so subtle ways. For example, as Miranda Fricker and others have shown, whiteness confers authority, whereas speaking from a non-white position is frequently perceived to discredit one's opinion. People of colour's views are deemed to be less neutral, to be biased and less reliable because of their race. This is why "genuinely free speech is an impossibility in a context where 'common sense' (what is rational and irrational) is determined by, and for, White people".[12]

The roots of the idea that defending the rights of racists to speak is not the same thing as defending those ideas is the First Amendment principle of viewpoint and content neutrality, the idea that all content is equally valid and that no authority—governmental or legal—has the right to pass judgment on any given speech. One of the results of this principle is that "racism is just another idea deserving of constitutional protection like all ideas".[13] Thus Laurence H. Tribe argues that "if the constitution forces government to allow people to march, speak, and write in favour of peace, then it must also require government to allow them to advocate hatred, racism, and even genocide".[14] One would have thought that such a line of reasoning would be an argument against the constitution and free speech absolutism; but evidently certain strands of constitutional fundamentalism lead to the view that somehow advocating for peace and advocating genocide are equivalent. If the consequences of sticking faithfully to a principle are that advocating hatred, racism and genocide are protected, then surely there is something wrong with either the principle or with sticking to it? There is a crucial difference between informed dissent—the right to criticise the powerful institutions that govern our lives—which happens to offend the powerful as it is perceived to threaten their power, and misinformed hate speech defending the powerful against the (structurally) weak. As Anshuman A. Mondal notes, "The words and actions of the powerful are not equivalent, either morally or politically, to those of the powerless".[15] More importantly, however, viewpoint and content neutrality are a myth. Critical race theorists, feminists and others have shown that the presumption of content neutrality masks all sorts of value judgements and ideological positions, and that content neutrality is impossible in structurally and discursively unequal societies. As Chris Demaske notes, the "legal system is riddled with value-based decisions", and it is difficult to see how it could not be.[16]

The argument that we must defend the right to express ideas we most strongly oppose is closely linked with the claim that "if the principle of free speech is curtailed, those with the least power are most likely to feel the chill".[17] Though this argument is repeatedly made, there is little evidence that it is true. Rather than worrying about a hypothetical situation in which something might or might not happen to those with the least power, why not look at what is happening to those with least power right now? In countries such as the United States, the United Kingdom and France, free speech cannot be said to be helping those with the least power. As Delgado and Stefancic argue, "Free speech is least helpful where we need it most", as it is "less able to deal with systemic social ills, such as racism or sexism, that are widespread and deeply woven into the fabric of society".[18] It is the case that in certain periods of history oppressed and marginalised groups have used free speech to try to advance their causes, but it is important to remember that at the same time they were using their free speech, so were others with contrary views, and often with greater access to louder more powerful platforms. Furthermore, for the most part free speech has served the dominant order; as Louis Seidman shows, "Over the course of [American] history, free speech law has only occasionally been of much help to progressive causes and during the modern period, it has been an important impediment".[19] This is not to dismiss the importance of free speech or campaigns for free speech in authoritarian regimes. In such contexts, free speech matters a great deal; however, it cannot be said that in today's liberal democracies free speech is a particularly effective tool against those with power—such as the media, corporations or governments. Indeed, the opposite is true. In the United States, for example, the large majority of exceptions to First Amendment protection favour the interests of the powerful.[20] As Seidman demonstrates, the First Amendment has been "a sword used by people at the apex of the American hierarchy of power".[21] And likewise, the common and dominant stories about free speech are propagated by powerful voices and institutions. Voices and institutions who have a vested interest in what Peters calls the "free speech story"—a mythical tale of heroic anti-conformist seekers of truth battling the dark forces of oppression. It is vital to recognise that free speech benefits power, and that free speech needs power—mostly financial power, but also the power of status and position—to be effective. As Seidman notes "because speech opportunities reflect current property distributions, free speech inherently favours people at the top of the power hierarchy".[22] In practice, this means that the rules of ownership trump the rights of expression. Indeed, free speech protection has increasingly been used by economic libertarians and corporate lawyers to empower corporations. Wendy Brown notes:

> In addition to empowering corporations to dominate the electoral process, as the infamous Citizens United decision did, the extension of free speech rights to corporations has been especially useful to the most disparaged quarters of big business: the pharmaceuticals, tobacco, coal, industrial meat, and airline industries have all made extensive use of free-speech challenges to advertising restrictions. It has also granted religious freedom to businesses that wish to spurn gay marriage or withhold employee insurance coverage for methods of birth control they believe to be un-Christian. The rubric is freedom, the ruse is corpora-

tions rendered as persons, and the project is rolling back restrictions and mandates of all kinds.[23]

This is particularly concerning, as the First Amendment of the US constitution plays a powerful and outsized role in establishing and legitimising dominant narratives about free speech in media discourses, both within and without the United States. It would be helpful if some of the scepticism directed towards the Second Amendment were also applied to the First. And it would be helpful if it was recognised that many of the people calling for absolute free speech are proponents of deregulation in all spheres; that free speech campaigns are often part of a broader ideological drive for economic liberalisation, for far-reaching deregulation and hence the erosion of, for example, environmental protection or worker's rights. The onslaught on regulation in speech has to be seen as part of wider onslaught on regulation more widely, an onslaught which has brought few benefits but caused devastating damage.

It is also important to recall that the United States, which, as commentators never cease repeating, has the most robust protection of free speech—which is to say, of offensive hate speech—has had and continues to have a deeply ambivalent relationship with freedom. As we saw in chapter 1, the "liberalism that grounds American democracy was founded on a definition of liberty that places property before human freedom and human needs: it permits (even promotes) various forms of unfree labour, dispossession, and subordination based on race and gender".[24] The United States has never been the land of the free and has always been happy to support totalitarian regimes abroad. Some members of US society are free, but many others are not. And not only in the sense in which it has the highest incarceration rate in the world—and that it is a deeply racialised and unjust system—but also in the sense in which the level of inequality is so egregious that any nominal freedom citizens may have is so empty as to be meaningless. Freedom today in the United States and elsewhere has been decoupled from the common good and any understanding of individual and social responsibility. Henry Giroux notes that in neoliberal societies freedom is

> largely organized according to the narrow notions of individual self-interest and limited to the freedom from constraints. Central to this concept is the freedom to pursue one's self-interests independently of larger social concerns. For individuals in a consumer society, this often means the freedom to shop, own guns, and define rights without regard to the consequences for others or the larger social order.[25]

Such a limited conception of freedom accords with the dominant account of freedom underpinning free speech arguments, the way speech rights are viewed solely in terms of the individual rather than in terms of the public good. However, if one recognises that this ideal of freedom is an ideological fantasy, used to promote individualism and consumerism, and to obscure the role of economic and structural power as determinants in social freedom, if we recognise that individuals only exist in and as social relations, relations which are anything but equal, then we will see that free speech operates to reinforce existing relations of power. What many free speech controversies demonstrate is that self-declared liberals choose white privilege over racial equality every time; they choose their freedom over the freedom of oppressed others. But if we care about larger social concerns, the common good and our responsibility towards others, especially the marginalised, excluded, and oppressed and their right not only to be heard but to live free and fulfilling lives, then we need a radically alternative conception of freedom and free speech.

NOTES

1. Catherine A. MacKinnon, "Foreword", in *Speech and Harm: Controversies over Free Speech*, ed. Ishani Maitra and Mary Kate McGowan (Oxford: Oxford University Press), xiv.
2. Brendan O'Neill, "From No Platform to Safe Space: A Crisis of Enlightenment", in *Unsafe Space: The Crisis of Free Speech on Campus*, ed. Tom Slater (London: Palgrave, 2016), 12.
3. Simon Lee, *The Cost of Free Speech* (London: Faber and Faber, 1990), 56.
4. Lee, "Cost", 41.
5. John Durham Peters, *Courting the Abyss: Free Speech and the Liberal Tradition* (Chicago: University of Chicago Press, 2005), 21.
6. Ibid.
7. Ibid.
8. Brian Leiter, "The Case against Free Speech", *Sydney Law Review* 38, no. 407 (2016): 409, 413.
9. P. G. Ingram, *Censorship and Free Speech: Some Philosophical Bearings* (Aldershot, UK: Ashgate, 2000), 1.
10. Lee, "Cost", 10.
11. Leiter, "Case Against", 417–18.
12. David Gillborn, "Risk-Free Racism: Whiteness and So-Called 'Free Speech'", *Wake Forest Law Review* 44 (2009): 555.
13. Charles R. Lawrence III, Mari J. Matsuda, Kimberlé Williams Crenshaw and Richard Delgado, "Introduction", in *Words That Wound: Critical Race Theory, Assaultive Speech, and the First Amendment*, ed. Charles R. Lawrence III, Mari J. Matsuda, Kimberlé Williams Crenshaw, Richard Delgado (London: Routledge, 1993), 54, ebook.
14. Laurence H. Tribe, *American Constitutional Law* (Mineola, NY: Foundation Press, 1988), 838.

15. Anshuman A. Mondal, *Islam and Controversy: The Politics of Free Speech after Rushdie* (London: Palgrave Macmillan, 2014), 31.

16. Chris Demaske, *Modern Power and Free Speech: Contemporary Culture and Issues of Equality* (Lanham, MD: Lexington Books, 2009), xiv.

17. Michelle Goldberg, "The Worst Time for the Left to Give Up on Free Speech", *New York Times*, June 10, 2016, https://www.nytimes.com/2017/10/06/opinion/liberals-free-speech.html.

18. Richard Delgaldo and Jean Stefancic, "Images of the Outsider in American Law and Culture: Can Free Expression Remedy Systemic Social Ills?" in *Critical Race Theory: The Cutting Edge*, ed. Richard Delgaldo and Jean Stefancic (Philadelphia: Temple University Press, 2013), 323.

19. See Louis Michael Seidman, "Can Free Speech Be Progressive?", *Columbia Law Review* 118 (2018), https://scholarship.law.georgetown.edu/facpub/2038

20. Delgaldo and Stefancic, "Images of the Outsider", 327.

21. Seidman, "Progressive", 10.

22. Ibid., 12.

23. Wendy Brown, "Neoliberalism's Frankenstein: Authoritarian Freedom in Twenty-First Century 'Democracies'", *Critical Times* 1, no. 1 (2018): 76.

24. Robin D. G. Kelley, "Coates and West in Jackson", *Boston Review*, December 22, 2017, http://bostonreview.net/race/robin-d-g-kelley-coates-and-west-jackson.

25. Henry Giroux, *Zombie Politics and Culture in the Age of Casino Capitalism* (New York: Peter Lang, 2011), 9.

Bibliography

Ahmed, Sara. "Against Students". *New Inquiry*, June 29, 2015. https://thenewinquiry.com/against-students.
Allen, Danielle. "Why Middlebury's Violent Response to Charles Murray Reminded Me of the Little Rock Nine". *Washington Post*, March 7, 2017. https://www.washingtonpost.com/opinions/why-middleburys-violent-response-to-charles-murray-reminded-me-of-the-little-rock-nine/2017/03/07.
American Association of University Professors. "On Trigger Warnings". AAUP, August 2014. https://www.aaup.org/report/trigger-warnings.
Anderson, Gary L., and Michael Ian Cohen. "The New Democratic Professional: Confronting Markets, Metric and Managerialism". https://www.unite4education.org/global-response/the-new-democratic-professional-confronting-markets-metrics-and-managerialism.
Ash, Timothy Garton. *Free Speech: Ten Principles for a Connected World*. London: Atlantic Book, 2016.
Bagehot. "Some Thoughts on the Crisis of Liberalism—and How to Fix It". *Economist*, June 12, 2018. https://www.economist.com/bagehots-notebook/2018/06/12/some-thoughts-on-the-crisis-of-liberalism-and-how-to-fix-it.
Beauchamp, Zack. "Data Shows a Surprising Campus Free Speech Problem: Left-Wingers Being Fired for Their Opinions". *Vox*, August 3, 2018. https://www.vox.com/policy-and-politics/2018/8/3/17644180/political-correctness-free-speech-liberal-data-georgetown.
———. "The New Reactionaries". *Vox*, February 26, 2019. https://www.vox.com/policy-and-politics/2019/2/26/18196429/trump-news-white-nationalism-hazony-kaufmann.
Bhambra, Gurminder K. "Brexit, Trump, and 'Methodological Whiteness': On the Misrecognition of Race and Class". *British Journal of Sociology*, 68, no. S1 (2017): S214–32.
Bhopal, Kalwant. *White Privilege: The Myth of a Post-racial Society*. Bristol, UK: Policy Press, 2018.
Biggar, Nigel. "Don't Feel Guilty about Our Colonial History". *Times*, November 30, 2017. https://www.thetimes.co.uk/article/don-t-feel-guilty-about-our-colonial-history.

"Broken Inquiry on Campus: A Response by a Collection of Middlebury Students". *Broken Inquiry on Campus* [blog], March 12, 2017. https://brokeninquiryblog.wordpress.com.

Brown, Wendy. "Neoliberalism's Frankenstein: Authoritarian Freedom in Twenty-First Century 'Democracies'". *Critical Times* 1, no. 1 (2019): 60–79.

———. *Regulating Aversion: Tolerance in the Age of Identity and Empire*. Princeton, NJ: Princeton University Press, 2006.

Busby, Eleanor. "Claims Students Have Created University Free Speech Crisis Have Been 'Exaggerated', Says Report". *Independent*, March 27, 2018. https://www.independent.co.uk/news/education/education-news/free-speech-students-uk-universities-human-rights-no-platforming-higher-education-a8276246.html.

Bush, George W. "President Bush Addresses the Nation". *Washington Post*, September 20, 2001. https://www.washingtonpost.com/wp-srv/nation/specials/attacked/transcripts/bushaddress_092001.html.

Carpenter, Bennett. "Free Speech, Black Lives and White Fragility". *Duke Chronicle*, January 19, 2016. https://www.dukechronicle.com/article/2016/01/free-speech-black-lives-and-white-fragility.

Cauce, Ana Mari. "Messy but Essential". *Inside Higher Ed*, November 20, 2017. https://www.insidehighered.com/views/2017/11/20/why-we-need-protect-free-speech-campuses-essay.

Césaire, Aimé. *Discourse on Colonialism*. New York: Monthly Review Press, 2000.

Chakrabarty, Dipesh. *Provincializing Europe: Postcolonial Thought and Historical Difference*. Princeton, NJ: Princeton University Press, 2000.

"Charles Murray at Middlebury: Unacceptable and Unethical, Say Over 500 Alumni", *Beyond the Green*, March 2, 2017. https://beyondthegreenmidd.wordpress.com/2017/03/02/charles-murray-at-middlebury-unacceptable-and-unethical-say-over-500-alumni/.

Citations Needed. "Episode 32: Attack of the PC College Kids!" Podcast. https://citationsneeded.libsyn.com/episode-32-attack-of-the-pc-college-kids.

———. Episode 74: "Liberal Ghandi Fetishism". Podcast. https://citationsneeded.libsyn.com/episode-74-liberal-gandhi-fetishism-and-the-problem-with-pop-notions-of-violence.

Cobb, Jelani. "Race and the Free Speech Diversion". *New Yorker*, November 10, 2015. https://www.newyorker.com/news/news-desk/race-and-the-free-speech-diversion.

Cohen, Joshua. "Freedom of Expression". *Philosophy and Public Affairs* 22, no. 3 (1993): 207–63.

Cohen, Richard. "Protesters at Middlebury College Demonstrate 'Cultural Appropriation'—of Fascism". *Washington Post*, May 29, 2017. https://www.washingtonpost.com/opinions/protesters-at-middlebury-college-demonstrate-cultural-appropriation--of-fascism/2017/05/29.

Cohort of Middlebury Professors. "Letter from Middlebury Faculty". *Middlebury Campus*, March 2, 2017. https://middleburycampus.com/35336/opinion/letter-from-middlebury-faculty.

Connell, Raewyn. "Ivory Tower and Market, the Silent Privatisation of Higher Education". Unite for Quality Education, August 22, 2018. https://www.unite4education.org/global-response/ivory-tower-market-the-silent-privatisation-of-higher-education.

Cooke, Charles C. W. "The New 'McCarthyism' Exists, but It Has Nothing to Do with Ted Cruz". *National Review*, March 25, 2015. http://www.nationalreview.com/article/415932/new-mccarthyism-exists-it-has-nothing-do-ted-cruz-charles-c-w-cooke.

Crenshaw, Kimberlé Williams. "Race Liberalism and the Deradicalization of Racial Reform". *Harvard Law Review*, 130 (2017): 2298.

———. "Mark Lilla's Comfort Zone". *Baffler*, September 14, 2017. https://thebaffler.com/latest/mark-lillas-comfort-zone.
Crouch, Colin. *Post-Democracy*. London: Polity, 2004.
Davies, Will. "The Free Speech Panic: How the Right Concocted a Crisis". *Guardian*, July 26, 2018. https://www.theguardian.com/news/2018/jul/26/the-free-speech-panic-censorship-how-the-right-concocted-a-crisis.
Dawes, Simon. "Charlie Hebdo and the Right to Offend". *openDemocracy*, January 21, 2015. https://www.opendemocracy.net/en/can-europe-make-it/charlie-hebdo-and-right-to-offend.
DeCew, Judith Wagner. "Free Speech and Offensive Expression". In *Freedom of Speech*, edited by Ellen Frankel Paul, Fred D. Miller Jr. and Jeffrey Paul, 81–103. Cambridge: Cambridge University Press, 2004.
De Genova, Nicholas. "The Whiteness of Innocence: *Charlie Hebdo* and the Metaphysics of Anti-Terrorism in Europe". In *After Charlie Hebdo : Terror, Racism and Free Speech*, edited by Gavan Titley, Des Freedman, Gholam Khiabany and Aurélien Mondon, 97–113. London: Zed Books, 2017.
Delgaldo, Richard, and Jean Stefancic. "Images of the Outsider in American Law and Culture: Can Free Expression Remedy Systemic Social Ills?" In *Critical Race Theory: The Cutting Edge*, edited by Richard Delgaldo and Jean Stefancic, 323–32. Philadelphia: Temple University Press, 2013.
Delphy, Christine. *Separate and Dominate*. London: Verso, 2012.
Demaske, Chris. *Modern Power and Free Speech: Contemporary Culture and Issues of Equality*. Lanham, MD: Lexington Books, 2009.
Deneen, Patrick J. *Why Liberalism Failed*. New Haven, CT: Yale University Press, 2018.
Denvir, Daniel, and Thea Riofrancos. "Zombie Liberalism". *n+1*, April 11, 2018. https://nplusonemag.com/online-only/online-only/zombie-liberalism.
DiAngelo, Robin. "White Fragility". *International Journal of Critical Pedagogy* 3, no. 3 (2011): 54–70.
"Discord at Middlebury: Students on the Anti-Murray Protests". *New York Times*, March 7, 2017. https://www.nytimes.com/2017/03/07/opinion/discord-at-middlebury-students-on-the-anti-murray-protests.html.
Du Bois, W. E. B. *The World and Africa*. New York: International Publishers, 1947.
Eatwell, Roger, and Matthew Goodwin. *National Populism: The Revolt against Liberal Democracy*. London: Pelican, 2018.
Fekete, Liz. *Europe's Fault Lines: Racism and the Rise of the Right*. London: Verso, 2018.
———. *A Suitable Enemy*. London: Pluto Press, 2009.
Ferguson, Niall. "Join My Nato or Watch Critical Thinking Die". *Sunday Times*, April 14, 2019. https://www.thetimes.co.uk/article/join-my-nato-or-watch-critical-thinking-die.
Fox, Claire. *"I Find That Offensive!"* London: Biteback, 2016.
François, Myriam. "The Fury of 'White People' with Jon Snow Shows a Total Lack of Self-Awareness on Race". *Guardian*, April 12, 2019. https://www.theguardian.com/commentisfree/2019/apr/12/jon-snow-white-people-brexit-rally.
Freedman, Des. "Media Power and the Framing of the *Charlie Hebdo* Attacks". In *After Charlie Hebdo: Terror, Racism and Free Speech*, edited by Gavan Titley, Des Freedman, Gholam Khiabany and Aurélien Mondon, 209–22. London: Zed Books, 2017.
Fricker, Miranda. *Epistemic Injustice: Power and the Ethics of Knowing*. Oxford: Oxford University Press, 2007.
Garner, Steve, and Saher Selod. "The Racialization of Muslims: Empirical Studies of Islamophobia". *Critical Sociology* 41, no. 1 (2015): 9–19.

Gee, Taylor. "How the Middlebury Riot Really Went Down". *Politico*, May 28, 2017. https://www.politico.com/magazine/story/2017/05/28/how-donald-trump-caused-the-middlebury-melee.
Gelber, Katherine. *Free Speech after 9/11*. Oxford: Oxford University Press, 2016.
Gillborn, David. "Risk-Free Racism: Whiteness and So-Called 'Free Speech'". *Wake Forest Law Review* 44 (2009): 535–55.
Ginsberg, Jodie. "The Right to Free Speech Means Nothing without the Right to Offend". *Guardian*, February 16, 2015. https://www.theguardian.com/commentisfree/2015/feb/16/free-speech-means-nothing-without-right-to-offend-paris-copenhagen.
Giroux, Henry. *Zombie Politics and Culture in the Age of Casino Capitalism*. New York: Peter Lang, 2011.
Goldberg, Michelle. "The Worst Time for the Left to Give up on Free Speech". *New York Times*, June 10, 2016. https://www.nytimes.com/2017/10/06/opinion/liberals-free-speech.html.
Goldfarb, Jeffrey C. "Free Speech Matters vs. Black Lives Matter". *Public Seminar*, September 29, 2017. http://www.publicseminar.org/2017/09/free-speech-matters-vs-black-lives-matter.
Gould, Jon. "Getting the Story Wrong on Campus Racism". *The Hill*, 17 November, 2015. https://thehill.com/blogs/pundits-blog/education/260379-getting-the-story-wrong-on-campus-racism.
Haidt, Jonathan. "The Age of Outrage". *City Journal*, December 17, 2017. https://www.city-journal.org/html/age-outrage-15608.html.
———. "The Fragile Generation". *Spiked*, September 1, 2017. http://www.spiked-online.com/spiked-review/article/the-fragile-generation/20257#.
Halliday, Fred. "'Islamophobia' Reconsidered". *Ethnic and Racial Studies*, 22 no. 5, (1999): 892–902.
Hanley, Lynsey. "Airtime for Hitler". *LRB Blog*. August 8, 2018. https://www.lrb.co.uk/blog/2018/august/airtime-for-hitler.
Harris, Malcolm. *Kids These Days: Human Capital and the Making of Millennials*. New York: Little Brown, 2018.
Hasan, Mehdi. "As a Muslim, I'm Fed Up with the Hypocrisy of the Free Speech Fundamentalists". *New Statesman*, December 1, 2015. https://www.newstatesman.com/mehdi-hasan/2015/01/muslim-i-m-fed-hypocrisy-free-speech-fundamentalists.
Hirsch, Afua. "The Fantasy of 'Free Speech'". *Prospect Magazine*, February 16, 2018. https://www.prospectmagazine.co.uk/politics/the-fantasy-of-free-speech.
Hitchens, Peter. "Free Speech Is under Threat over Islamophobia". *Times*, March 26, 2019.
Howarth, Alan. *Free Speech*. London: Routledge, 1998.
Hume, Mick. *Trigger Warning: Is the Fear of Being Offensive Killing Free Speech?* London: William Collins, 2015.
Hutton, Will. "Cecil Rhodes Was a Racist, But You Can't Readily Expunge Him from History". *Guardian*, December 20, 2015. https://www.theguardian.com/commentisfree/2015/dec/20/atonement-for-the-past-not-censorship-of-history.
Ingram, P. G. *Censorship and Free Speech: Some Philosophical Bearings*. Aldershot, UK: Ashgate, 2000.
Jenkins, Simon. "Pale Stale Males Are the Last Group It's OK to Vilify". *Guardian*, December 15, 2016. https://www.theguardian.com/commentisfree/2016/dec/15/pale-stale-males-blamed-brexit-trump.
Kapoor, Nisha. *Deport, Deprive, Extradite: 21st Century State Extremism*. London: Verso, 2018.
Kauffman, Eric. "How Progressivism Enabled the Rise of the Populist Right". *Quillette*, May 27, 2019. https://quillette.com/2019/05/27/how-progressivism-enabled-the-rise-of-the-populist-right.

Kelley, Robin D. G. "Black Study, Black Struggle". *Boston Review*, March 7, 2016. http://bostonreview.net/forum/robin-d-g-kelley-black-study-black-struggle.
———. "Coates and West in Jackson". *Boston Review*, December 22, 2017. http://bostonreview.net/race/robin-d-g-kelley-coates-and-west-jackson.
———. "Identity Politics and Class Struggle". *New Politics*, 6, no. 2 (1997). https://libcom.org/library/identity-politics-class-struggle.
———. "Introduction: A Poetics of Anti-Colonialism". In *Discourse on Colonialism*. By Aimé Césaire, 7–28. New York: Monthly Review Press, 2000.
Kennedy, Joe. *Authentocrats*. London: Repeater, 2018.
Kent, Martin. "Roger Scruton Claims He Is the Victim of a 'Right Wing Witch Hunt' as Row over New Statesman Interview Continues". *INews*, April 26, 2019. https://inews.co.uk/news/roger-scruton-george-eaton-new-statesman-spectator-interview-bbc-today-programme.
Kobek, Jarett. *I Hate the Internet*. London: Serpent's Tale, 2016.
Kumar, Deepa. "Islamophobia and Empire: An Intermestic Approach to the Study of Anti-Muslim Racism". In *What Is Islamophobia? Racism, Social Movements and the State*, edited by Narzanin Massoumi, Tom Mills and David Miller, 49–73. London: Pluto Press, 2017.
Kundnani, Arun. "Islamophobia as Ideology of US Empire". In *What Is Islamophobia? Racism, Social Movements and the State*, edited by Narzanin Massoumi, Tom Mills and David Miller, 35–48. London: Pluto Press, 2017.
———. "Islamophobia: Lay-Ideology of US-Led Empire". www.kundnani.org/wp-content/uploads/Kundnani-Islamophobia-as-lay-ideology-of-US- empire.pdf.
———. *'The Muslims Are Coming!'* London: Verso, 2015.
Lawrence, Charles R. III, Mari J. Matsuda, Kimberlé Williams Crenshaw, Richard Delgado, eds. *Words That Wound: Critical Race Theory, Assaultive Speech, and the First Amendment*. London: Routledge, 1993.
Lean, Nathan C. "Mainstreaming Anti-Muslim Prejudice: The Rise of the Islamophobia Industry in American Electoral Politics". In *What Is Islamophobia? Racism, Social Movements and the State*, ed. Narzanin Massoumi, Tom Mills and David Miller, 123–36. London: Pluto Press, 2017.
Lee, Simon. *The Cost of Free Speech*. London: Faber and Faber, 1990.
Lee, Stewart. "Why Greta Thunberg Is Now My Go-to Girl". *Guardian*, April 28, 2019. https://www.theguardian.com/commentisfree/2019/apr/28/why-greta-thunberg-is-now-my-go-to-girl.
Leiter, Brian. "The Case against Free Speech", *Sydney Law Review*, 38 no. 407 (2016): 409, 413.
Lilla, Mark. "The End of Identity Liberalism". *New York Times*, November 18, 2016. https://www.nytimes.com/2016/11/20/opinion/sunday/the-end-of-identity-liberalism.html.
Losurdo, Domenico. *Liberalism: A Counter-History*. London: Verso, 2014.
Lukianoff, Greg, and Jonathan Haidt. "The Coddling of the American Mind", *Atlantic*, September 2015. https://www.theatlantic.com/magazine/archive/2015/09/the-coddling-of-the-american-mind.
MacKinnon, Catherine A. "Foreword". In *Speech and Harm: Controversies over Free Speech*, ed. Ishani Maitra and Mary Kate McGowan, vi–xviii. Oxford: Oxford University Press, 2012.
Maitra, Ishani. "Subordinating Speech". In *Speech and Harm: Controversies over Free Speech*, edited by Maitra, Ishani, and Mary Kate McGowan, 94–118. Oxford: Oxford University Press, 2012.
Maitra, Ishani, and Mary Kate McGowan, eds. *Speech and Harm: Controversies over Free Speech*. Oxford: Oxford University Press, 2012.

Mamdani, Mahmood. *Good Muslim, Bad Muslim: America, The Cold War, and the Roots of Terror*. New York: Three Leaves Press, 2005.
Manzoor-Khan, Suhaiymah. *Postcolonial Banter*. Birmingham, UK: Verve Poetry Press, 2019.
Marlière, Philippe. "The Meaning of 'Charlie': The Debate on the Troubled French Identity". In *After Charlie Hebdo: Terror, Racism and Free Speech*, edited by Gavan Titley, Des Freedman, Gholam Khiabany and Aurélien Mondon, 46–62. London: Zed Books, 2017.
Massoumi, Narzanin, Tom Mills and David Miller. "Liberal and Left Movements and the Rise of Islamophobia". In *What Is Islamophobia? Racism, Social Movements and the State*, 234–69. London: Pluto Press, 2017.
———, eds. *What Is Islamophobia? Racism, Social Movements and the State*. London: Pluto Press, 2017.
Mari J. Matsuda, "Public Response to Racist Speech: Considering the Victim's Story". In *Words That Wound: Critical Race Theory, Assaultive Speech, and the First Amendment*, edited by Charles R. Lawrence III, Mari J. Matsuda, Kimberlé Williams Crenshaw, and Richard Delgado, 17–52. London: Routledge, 1993.
McMahan, Jeff, Francesca Minerva and Peter Singer, "Setting the Record Straight on the '*Journal of Controversial Ideas*'". *Guardian*, November 18, 2018. https://www.theguardian.com/world/2018/nov/18/setting-the-record-straight-on-the-journal-of-controversial-ideas.
Mcquillan, Martin. "Gyimah's Freedom of Speech Claims under Scrutiny Again". *Research Professional*, June 29, 2018. https://www.researchresearch.com/news/article/?articleId=1375991.
Mehta, Uday Singh. *Liberalism and Empire: A Study in Nineteenth-Century British Liberal Thought*. Chicago: University of Chicago, 1999.
"Middlebury's Statement of Principle". *Wall Street Journal*, March 6, 2017. https://www.wsj.com/articles/middleburys-statement-of-principle-1488846993.
Mill, J. S. *On Liberty*. Edited by Stefan Collini. Cambridge: Cambridge University Press, 1989.
Miller, M. H. "The Inescapable Weight of My $100000 Student Debt". *Guardian*, August 21, 2018. https://www.theguardian.com/news/2018/aug/21/the-inescapable-weight-of-my-100000-student-debt.
Mills, Charles W. *Black Rights/White Wrongs: The Critique of Racial Liberalism*. Oxford: Oxford University Press, 2017.
———. *The Racial Contract*. Ithaca, NY: Cornell University Press, 1997.
Mishra, Pankaj. "The Mask It Wears". *London Review of Books*, June 21, 2018. https://www.lrb.co.uk/v40/n12/pankaj-mishra/the-mask-it-wears.
Mishra, Pankaj. "The Religion of Whiteness Becomes a Suicide Cult". *New York Times*, August 30, 2018. https://www.nytimes.com/2018/08/30/opinion/race-politics-whiteness.html.
Mitropolous, Angela. "B-Grade Politics". *Medium*, November 23, 2013. https://medium.com/i-m-h-o/b-grade-politics.
Monbiot, George. "How US Billionaires Are Fuelling the Hard-Right Cause in Britain". *Guardian*, December 7, 2018. https://www.theguardian.com/commentisfree/2018/dec/07/us-billionaires-hard-right-britain-spiked-magazine-charles-david-koch-foundation.
Mondal, Anshuman A. *Islam and Controversy: The Politics of Free Speech after Rushdie*. London: Palgrave Macmillan, 2014.
Mondon, Aurélien, and Aaron Winter. "*Charlie Hebdo*, Republican Secularism and Islamophobia". In *After Charlie Hebdo: Terror, Racism and Free Speech*, edited by Gavan Titley, Des Freedman, Gholam Khiabany and Aurélien Mondon, 31–45. London: Zed Books, 2017.

———. "Understanding the Mainstreaming of the Far Right". *openDemocracy*, August 26, 2018. https://www.opendemocracy.net/en/can-europe-make-it/understanding-mainstreaming-of-far-right.

Morsi, Yassir. *Radical Skin, Moderate Masks: De-radicalising the Muslim and Racism in Post-racial Societies*. London: Rowman & Littlefield, 2017.

Mounk, Yascha. "How Populist Uprisings Could Bring Down Liberal Democracy". *Guardian*, March 4, 2018. https://www.theguardian.com/commentisfree/2018/mar/04/shock-system-liberal-democracy-populism.

Muller, Jerry Z. "The Tyranny of Metrics: The Quest to Quantify Everything Undermines Higher Education". *Chronicle of Higher Education*, January 21, 2018. https://www.chronicle.com/article/The-Tyranny-of-Metrics/242269.

"New Oxford Vice-Chancellor Urges 'Open-Minded' Students". BBC, January 12, 2016. https://www.bbc.co.uk/news/uk-england-oxfordshire-35290156.

Newey, Glen. "Unlike a Scotch Egg". *London Review of Books*, December 5, 2013. https://www.lrb.co.uk/v35/n23/glen-newey/unlike-a-scotch-egg.

Nielsen, Laura Beth. "Power in Public: Reactions, Responses, and Resistance to Offensive Public Speech". In *Speech and Harm: Controversies over Free Speech*, edited by Ishani Maitra and Mary Kate McGowan, 148–73. Oxford: Oxford University Press, 2012.

O'Neill, Brendan. "From No Platform to Safe Space: A Crisis of Enlightenment". In *Unsafe Space: The Crisis of Free Speech on Campus*, edited by Tom Slater, 5–21. London: Palgrave, 2016.

———. "Restore the Right to Offend". *Brendan O'Neill* [blog], January 9, 2015. https://brendanoneill.co.uk/post/107600481429/restore-the-right-to-offend.

"Oxford Uni Don Says 'Peer Pressure' Is Stifling Debate". BBC, February 2, 2018. https://www.bbc.co.uk/news/uk-england-oxfordshire-42887083.

Pape, Robert. *Dying to Win: The Strategic Logic of Suicide Terrorism*. New York: Random House 2006.

Patel, Vimal. "Yes, Students at Sarah Lawrence Are Demanding Free Detergent. But There's More to It Than You Might Think". *Chronicle of Higher Education*, March 15, 2019. https://www.chronicle.com/article/Yes-Students-at-Sarah/245913.

Paul, Ellen Frankel, Fred D. Miller Jr. and Jeffrey Paul, eds. *Freedom of Speech*. Cambridge: Cambridge University Press, 2004.

Paul, Joshua. "'Not Black and White, but Black and Red': Anti-identity Identity Politics and #AllLivesMatter". *Ethnicities* 1, 19 (2019): 3–19.

PEN America. *And Campus for All: Diversity, Inclusion and Freedom of Speech at U.S. Universities*. New York: PEN America, 2016. https://pen.org/wp-content/uploads/2017/06/PEN_campus_report_06.15.2017.pdf.

"The People vs 'the Elite'? State of Hate 2019". Hope Not Hate. https://www.hopenothate.org.uk/research/state-of-hate-report-2019/.

Peters, John Durham. *Courting the Abyss: Free Speech and the Liberal Tradition*. Chicago: University of Chicago Press, 2005.

Peterson, Jennifer. "Freedom of Expression as Liberal Fantasy: The Debate over *The People vs. Larry Flynt*. *Media, Culture & Society* 29, no. 3 (2007): 377–94.

Pollock, Griselda. *Vision and Difference*. London: Routledge, 1988.

Purdy, Jedediah. "Normcore". *Dissent*, Summer 2018. https://www.dissentmagazine.org/article/normcore-trump-resistance-books-crisis-of-democracy.

Rana, Aziz. *The Two Faces of American Freedom*. Cambridge, MA: Harvard University Press, 2010.

Ravndal, Jacob Aasland. "Explaining Right-Wing Terrorism and Violence in Western Europe: Grievances, Opportunities and Polarization". *European Journal of Political Research* 57 (2018): 845–66.

Reimer, Nick. "Weaponising Learning". *Sydney Review of Books*, June 12, 2018. https://sydneyreviewofbooks.com/weaponising-learning.

Roberts, David. "American White People Really Hate Being Called 'White People'". *Vox*. https://www.vox.com/policy-and-politics/2018/7/26/17613844/racial-diversity-poll-twitter-white-people.

Robinson, Nathan J. "Let's Just Stop Writing Long-Form Profiles of Nazis". *Current Affairs*, November 27, 2017. https://www.currentaffairs.org/2017/11/lets-just-stop-writing-long-form-profiles-of-nazis.

Rogers, Katie. "Pro-Trump Chalk Messages Cause Conflicts on College Campuses". *New York Times*, April 1, 2016. https://www.nytimes.com/2016/04/02/us/pro-trump-chalk-messages-cause-conflicts-on-college-campuses.html.

Roth, Michael. "Inequality and the 'Once and Future Liberal'". *Inside Higher Ed*, August 31, 2017. https://www.insidehighered.com/views/2017/08/31/reflection-mark-lillas-essay-and-book-about-identity-politics-essay.

Saini, Angela. "Why Race Science Is on the Rise Again". *Guardian*, May 18, 2019. https://www.theguardian.com/books/2019/may/18/race-science-on-the-rise-angela-saini.

Sandbrook, Dominic. "Of Course Slavery Was Abhorrent. But Cambridge Dons Who Now Feel Guilty about Our Empire Are Narcissistic Cowards". *Mail Online*, May 1, 2019. https://www.dailymail.co.uk/debate/article-6978591.

Schauer, Frederick. "On the Distinction between Speech and Action". *Emory Law Journal* 65, no. 2 (2015): 427–54.

Schlosser, Edward. "I'm a Liberal Professor, and My Liberal Students Terrify Me". *Vox*, June 3, 2015. https://www.vox.com/2015/6/3/8706323/college-professor-afraid.

Scott, Joan. "On Free Speech and Academic Freedom". *AAUP Journal of Academic Freedom* 8 (2017): 1–10.

Seidman, Louis Michael. "Can Free Speech Be Progressive?", *Columbia Law Review* 118 (2018): 1–30.

Shackle, Samira. "'The Way Universities Are Run Is Making Us Ill': Inside the Student Mental Health Crisis". *Guardian*, 27 September, 2019. https://www.theguardian.com/society/2019/sep/27/anxiety-mental-breakdowns-depression-uk-student.

Slater, Tom. "Introduction: Reinvigorating the Spirit of '64". In *Unsafe Space: The Crisis of Free Speech on Campus*, edited by Tom Slater, 1–4. London: Palgrave, 2016.

Sleeper, Jim. "The Conservatives Behind the Campus 'Free Speech' Crusade". *American Prospect*, October 19, 2016. http://prospect.org/article/conservatives-behind-campus-'free-speech'-crusade.

———. "Political Correctness and Its Real Enemies". *New York Times*, September 3, 2016. https://www.nytimes.com/2016/09/04/opinion/sunday/political-correctness-and-its-real-enemies.html.

———. "What the Campus 'Free Speech' Crusade Won't Say". *AlterNet* September 4, 2016. https://www.alternet.org/education/what-campus-free-speech-crusade-wont-say.

Small, Mike. "Revealed: US Oil Billionaire Charles Koch Funds UK Anti-Environment Spiked Network". *Desmog*, December 7, 2018. https://www.desmog.co.uk/2018/12/04/spiked-lm-dark-money-koch-brothers.

Snyder, Jeffrey Aaron. "Free Speech? Now, That's Offensive". *Inside Higher Ed*, September 1, 2016. https://www.insidehighered.com/views/2016/09/01/dangers-not-valuing-free-speech-campuses-essay.

Souvlis, George. "Marxism, the Far-Right and the Antinomies of Liberalism: An interview with Enzo Traverso". Verso Books blog. https://www.versobooks.com/blogs/4296-marxism-the-far-right-and-the-antinomies-of-liberalism-an-interview-with-enzo-traverso.

Speri, Alice. "The Threat Within". *Intercept*, March 23, 2019. https://theintercept.com/2019/03/23/black-identity-extremist-fbi-domestic-terrorism.

Stanger, Allison. "Understanding the Angry Mob at Middlebury That Gave Me a Concussion". March 13, 2017, *New York Times*. https://www.nytimes.com/2017/03/13/opinion/understanding-the-angry-mob-that-gave-me-a-concussion.html.

Staub, Michael E. "The Mismeasure of Minds". *Boston Review*, May 8, 2019. http://bostonreview.net/race/michael-e-staub-mismeasure-minds.

Taylor, Keeanga-Yamahtta. *From #BlackLivesMatter to Black Liberation*. Chicago: Haymarket Books, 2016.

Telegraph Reporters. "Universities Told They 'Must Commit to Free Speech' under New Plans". *Telegraph*, October 19, 2017. http://www.telegraph.co.uk/news/2017/10/19/universities-told-must-commit-free-speech-new-plans.

Tirrell, Lynne. "Genocidal Language Games". In *Speech and Harm: Controversies over Free Speech*, ed. Ishani Maitra and Mary Kate McGowan, 174–221. Oxford: Oxford University Press, 2012.

Toscano, Alberto. *Fanaticism*. London: Verso, 2017.

Tribe, Laurence H. *American Constitutional Law*. Mineola, NY: Foundation Press, 1988.

Turner, Janice. "How Political Editor Laura Kuenssberg Broke the Mould to Become the BBC's Brexit Guru". *Times*, March 30, 2019. https://www.thetimes.co.uk/article/how-political-editor-laura-kuenssberg-broke-the-mould-to-become-the-bbcs-brexit-guru-0lp9qhl2f.

Weigel, Moira. "*The Coddling of the American Mind* Review—How Elite US Liberals Have Turned Rightwards", *Guardian*, 20 September, 2018. https://www.theguardian.com/books/2018/sep/20/the-coddling-of-the-american-mind-review.

———. "Political Correctness: How the Right Invented a Phantom Enemy". *Guardian*, 30 November, 2016. https://www.theguardian.com/news/audio/2016/dec/19/political-correctness-how-the-right-invented-a-phantom-enemy-podcast.

Wittgenstein, Ludwig. *Blue and Brown Books*. Oxford: Blackwell, 1958.

Wolfe, Patrick. *Traces of History: Elementary Structures of Race*. London: Verso, 2016.

Younge, Gary. "White Supremacy Feeds on Mainstream Encouragement. That Has to Stop". *Guardian*, April 5, 2019. https://www.theguardian.com/commentisfree/2019/apr/05/white-supremacy.

Zelizer, Julian E., and Morton Keller. "Is Free Speech Really Challenged on Campus?" *Atlantic*, September 15, 2017. https://www.theatlantic.com/education/archive/2017/09/students-free-speech-campus-protest.

Index

Austin, J. L., 77, 79

Bhmabra, Gurminder K., 21–23
Bell Curve, The, 65, 66
Brown, Wendy, 89, 90, 96

Charlie Hebdo, 91–94
"The Coddling of the American Mind", 41
critical race theory, 10, 63
Crouch, Colin, 13
culture war, 4, 35, 40, 41

Delgado, Richard, and Stefancic, Jean, 67
democracy, 1, 5, 13, 15, 43, 49, 52, 85
DiAngelo, Robin, 74–75

enlightenment values, 23, 25

far right, 2, 5, 17, 19, 20, 85
Fekete, Liz, 20, 101
feminist philosophy of language, 63
first amendment, 11, 29, 73, 77, 110–113
Fricker, Miranda, 45, 110

Garton Ash, Timothy, 74–75

Haidt, Jonathan, 15, 16, 21, 28–29; and Lukianoff, Greg, 41
hard-working white man, 17, 19, 21
Harris, Malcolm, 51
House of Commons, 43
Hutton, Will, 62

identity politics, 4, 15, 18, 23, 24, 25

Johnson, Jo, 42, 45, 46

Kelley, Robin D. G., 25
Kids These Days, 51
Kundnani, Arun, 86

Langton, Rae, 79
"left behind", 14, 17, 21, 23
liberal, 7, 75; anti-PC, 5, 17, 19, 21, 40, 83, 99; centre, 7, 17, 20; centrists, 14, 15, 17, 18, 21, 23, 72; commentariat, 47; democracy, 1, 9, 10, 13, 14, 15, 16, 29, 30, 70, 101; establishment, 4, 62, 63, 75; multiculturalism, 14, 23; values, 5, 101; white, 64, 74
liberalism, 3, 4, 6, 7, 8, 10, 13, 14, 16, 25–27, 59, 70, 75, 89, 90; crisis of, 10, 13; racial, 59, 73

127

libertarianism, 8
libertarians, 7, 18, 36, 40, 53, 75, 92
Losurdo, Domenico, 27

Middlebury College, 10, 61, 65;
    students, 69
Mill, John Stuart, 7, 8, 99
Mills, Charles W., 28, 59
Mondal, Anshuman, 97–98
moral panic, 4, 18, 40
Mounk, Yascha, 16, 25, 26
Murray, Charles, 10, 61, 65–66, 70, 72

new atheists, 90
neoliberalism, 11, 13, 14, 51
no platforming, 46, 49

Office for Students, 42
On Liberty, 8, 74

PEN America, 36, 40, 62–63

Radical Skin/Moderate Masks, 100
Rana, Aziz, 29–30

safe space, 46, 49
Schlosser, Edward, 38, 52
slavery, 27
Spiked, 18, 40, 76
Stanger, Allison, 65–66, 66, 70, 71

Tirrell, Lynne, 78

white fragility, 64
white supremacy, 4, 8, 10, 19, 23, 30,
    59, 64, 66, 70, 93
Wittgenstein, Ludwig, 3, 77, 95
Woolf, Patrick, 28
Words That Wound, 40

Younge, Gary, 20

www.ingramcontent.com/pod-product-compliance
Lightning Source LLC
Chambersburg PA
CBHW030241170426
43202CB00007B/80